healthy recipes
for your
steamer

carolyn humphries

foulsham

LONDON • NEW YORK • TORONTO • SYDNEY

foulsham

The Publishing House, Bennetts Close, Cippenham,
Slough, Berkshire, SL1 5AP, England

ISBN-13: 978-0-572-03156-5
ISBN-10: 0-572-03156-4

Cover photograph by Karen Thomas. Home Economist: Valerie Berry

The moral right of the author has been asserted

A CIP record for this book is available from the British Library

Previously published as *Real Food Recipes for Your Steamer*

Thanks to Tefal for supplying a Steam Cuisine 900 Turbo Diffusion
for testing the recipes

Printed in Great Britain by Mackays of Chatham plc, Chatham, Kent

Contents

Introduction

Steaming is a fantastically healthy, versatile and simple way to cook. It's not new, however. Man was steaming food even before he discovered fire, cooking over hot springs or in leaves on hot stones. The ancient Chinese created bamboo baskets to steam delicate foods and these are still widely used today. But now you can choose from a whole array of gadgets in which to steam-cook. There are specially designed steamers – from streamlined electric to shiny chrome tiered ones – or you can simply use two plates or a colander over a saucepan of boiling water. This book tells you how to use all these methods.

Steaming is a moist, delicious method of cooking. Forget any ideas you may have of bland 'invalid' food – steaming produces glorious colours, flavours and textures in everything you eat. With this book you can learn to create whole meals in a stack; smooth, velvety sauces; light, luscious puddings; vibrant, tasty vegetables and fruits; perfectly produced cheese and egg dishes and tender, succulent meat, fish and poultry. You'll also discover how to make the fluffiest rice and couscous and non-sticky pasta. Steaming is a wonderful way to cook because, for the most part, the food cooks without any attention from you – you leave it to do its own thing. It's ideal for the health-conscious, as you don't have to add any extra fat (unless you want to) and it can save on fuel costs too, as you can cook a whole meal in one stack of tiers.

With this great range of exciting new recipes – and a complete section on good old traditional favourites too – you can be sure you will enjoy a fabulous, all-round culinary experience!

Steaming – the healthy option

Vitamins and minerals are lost as soon as cut surfaces of vegetables and fruit are exposed to air or water. But if you cook in steam the loss is reduced, so many more nutrients are retained – together with the lovely bright colours and intense flavours (which are diluted by cooking in water). For instance, when you steam broccoli, you retain nearly three-quarters of the vitamin C whereas if you boil it, you **lose** almost two-thirds! Other foods, too, benefit from this method. Steamed brown rice, for example, keeps nearly all its vitamin B1, which is lost with other cooking methods. Meat, fish and poultry, which lose some vitamin A, in particular, when they are cooked at high temperatures, retain far more nutrients when steamed, and the gentle cooking method also helps to soften the fibres, making them tender, moist and easily digestible.

To maximise the health value, if steaming in a dish, try serving the cooking juices with the food, either just as they are or made into a sauce. But remember, too, if you use a steamer to reheat food, some nutrients will inevitably be lost.

How steaming works

The principles of steaming are the same whichever type of gadget you use. Steam is created by boiling liquid in the base container. It rises up through the food lying in a perforated container suspended above the liquid. The boiling liquid itself never comes into direct contact with the food.

There may be several steamer tiers, stacked snugly on top of each other, and the top is sealed with a tight-fitting lid. This prevents the steam from escaping, but allows it to circulate round the food, cooking it in the heat and moisture. The further the food is away from the source of the steam, the less steam there will be, thus lengthening the cooking time. For this reason, you should always put denser foods that need more cooking in the bottom tiers, close to the steam source, and tender, delicate foods that require less cooking in the top tiers.

When using basins or other covered containers of food, make sure there is enough room inside the cover to allow for rising (of steamed puddings etc.) or for the accumulation of cooking juices.

Steaming methods

As I said earlier, there are several different ways to steam.

Method 1
The food is placed in a perforated container and suspended over boiling water.

Whether you use an electric steamer, stacking metal or bamboo tiers or an expanding steamer, this is the method for most steam cookery. The food is placed directly in the container and covered tightly with a lid. No water comes into contact with the food at all. It is suitable for cooking meats, poultry, fish, vegetables, fruit and light desserts.

Method 2
The food is placed in a covered basin or in a foil-wrapped parcel or between two plates, over a pan of boiling water. Alternatively, a double saucepan may be used, with the water in the lower pan.

This method is suitable for making sauces, melting chocolate and steaming puddings, terrines, fillets of fish, chicken etc. It can also be used to reheat plated meals, to thaw some foods and to keep foods such as pancakes warm.

Again the food does not come in contact with the boiling water at all so the heat remains the same throughout the cooking process.

Method 3
The food is placed in a basin or other dish, which is then covered with a double thickness of foil or greaseproof (waxed) paper, twisted and folded under the rim to secure. Alternatively, a pudding cloth may be used to cover the basin, tied tightly with string. The basin is placed on a trivet (to prevent contact with the fierce heat at the base of the saucepan) in a pan of

boiling water, with enough water to come halfway up the sides of the basin. The pan is covered with a tight-fitting lid and the pan is topped up with more boiling water as it evaporates. It is vital that no moisture is allowed to touch the food or the results will be soggy and disappointing.

Method 4

This is similar to method 3. The food is placed in a bain marie, a shallow container in which dishes of delicate foods such as egg-based desserts may be steamed. Boiling water is added to come no more than halfway up the sides of the dishes of food. The whole water bath is covered with foil to contain the steam and the food is then simmered gently on the hob or cooked in the oven at no more than 160°C/325°F/gas mark 3 (fan oven 145°C).

Method 5

This is known as the absorption method and is particularly suitable for rice and other grains. The food is added to a measured amount of boiling water or stock in a pan. It is then brought back to the boil, covered tightly and the heat turned down as low as possible. The grain cooks and swells, first in the liquid and then, as the liquid is absorbed, in the resultant steam.

Types of Steamer

*T*here are several different kinds of steamer. They all cook in the same way, and their cooking times are much the same but do check manufacturer's guidelines for specialist models.

Electric steamers

These usually have a reservoir for water in the base, with two or more transparent tiers with perforated bases that stack on top. Some have a rice/sauce bowl that fits on the top or in between. Electric steamers have a timer and thermostat to ensure excellent cooking results. They also usually have a drip tray to catch cooking juices, which can then be used to make a sauce to serve with the finished dish (although this cooking liquid tends to be watery as it gets diluted by steam).

Electric steamers are particularly good as the tiers usually have removable bases, giving a larger cooking area when necessary. Also they automatically switch off if the water level drops too low and there is a reservoir level indicator so you can check when it needs topping up. Mind you, if you forget to check, and the cooker stops cooking, the timer also cuts out, which can be irritating if you can't remember how long you've been steaming for! For some people, the fact that the machines are quite big is a minus – they need to be kept on the work surface. However, you may consider this to be a plus because it leaves the actual hob free for other cooking when required. You must remember that only water may be put in the reservoir – you cannot add other foods to be cooked in this water.

Tiered metal steaming containers

These are usually made of stainless steel. They comprise two or more tiers with bases designed to sit neatly on top of your own saucepans, with a tight-fitting lid to seal the top tier. Water or other cooking liquid is boiled in the saucepan and foods are steamed in the various tiers. The main advantage over an electric steamer is that foods can be cooked actually in the liquid in the saucepan as well as in the tiers. Other fragrant flavourings can be added to the water, too, so the flavours permeate the steamed foods. The main disadvantage is that it is easy to boil the pan dry, so you have to remember to keep checking every so often.

Expanding metal containers

These are inexpensive and very useful. The sides of the containers open up in a fan shape to fit over different-sized saucepans – they look a bit like an upturned umbrella – and the lid from the saucepan fits over the top to create a seal. They take up very little storage space, but you can only use one per saucepan.

Metal colanders

Ordinary metal colanders work perfectly well as steamer containers, providing you have a saucepan on which the colander will fit snugly. The main disadvantage is that the bowl of the colander may go quite a long way down into the saucepan so you must take care that the boiling liquid does not come in direct contact with the food or you may get disappointing results.

Note: Never use a plastic colander as a steamer – it will melt!

Bamboo baskets

These original Chinese steamers work on exactly the same principal as the metal ones. They can be stacked and used over a saucepan or stood in a wok. If in a wok, the water must not come above the bamboo grille in the base. Their main advantage is that they are attractive enough to serve the food in at the table. However, they tend to be smaller than the metal ones and they are also less durable.

Wok and rack

This is the other traditional Chinese steaming method. The wok is part-filled with boiling water or stock and foods are laid on the rack suspended from the lip of the wok. The lid is put on and food is steamed in the normal way. The main advantage is that foods can be cooked in the liquid in the wok itself at the same time. The main disadvantage is that there is not as much room as in the stacking tiers.

Bowl over a saucepan or double saucepan

This is the ideal way to melt chocolate and to make egg-based sauces, such as Hollandaise or custard, which would curdle if they came into contact with a direct heat source. The food is placed in the bowl (or in the top saucepan if you are using a double saucepan) over the pan of simmering water, then stirred or whisked constantly until melted or thickened.

Two plates

This method is perhaps the simplest of all and has the great advantage that it requires no special equipment. The food is laid on one plate (with or without some liquid). This is placed on top of a saucepan of boiling water. A second plate of the same size is inverted over the top of the food, which is then steamed in the usual way. This is a particularly good way of reheating plated meals, steaming fish and keeping items such as pancakes warm.

Tips for Perfect Steaming

◇ Always choose top-quality foods. Steaming enhances all flavours and aromas – even the unpleasant ones – so only use it for fresh, unblemished vegetables, lean meats and fruit that is just ripe but never over-ripe.

◇ Choose foods of the same size or cut them into even-sized pieces, when necessary, so they take the same time to cook.

◇ Make sure there is enough space in the steamer to allow the steam to circulate all round the food.

◇ Arrange foods in an even layer. If they are mounded up or tightly packed, they will take much longer to cook.

◇ Always defrost meat, fish and poultry before steaming.

◇ Ensure the lid of the steamer is a secure fit so steam does not escape.

◇ Top up with boiling water or cooking liquid as necessary to prevent it boiling dry. Unless you are using an electric steamer, you should never add cold water or the temperature will drop, steam will be reduced, cooking time will be lengthened and texture and colour may be spoiled.

◇ If using plain water for steaming (and not adding foods to cook in the water), add a little lemon juice or vinegar. This will prevent the pan from discolouring during long periods of steaming.

◇ Never let the steaming liquid in the base of the steamer come into direct contact with the foods being steamed or the results will be soggy and disappointing.

◇ At the end of cooking time, check to see if the food is done. If not cooked to your liking, steam for longer.

◇ If using a tiered steamer, put the foods that take the longest cooking time in the bottom tiers and the more delicate ones in the top tiers. If necessary, add foods that take a shorter time when the other foods are partially cooked.

Cooking a complete meal in a steamer

It is perfectly possible to cook a complete meal, using an electric steamer or a tiered steamer over a saucepan. Always remember that the foods that take longest to cook should be in the bottom tiers and should be put on to cook first. You then add the other foods in other tiers later to ensure everything is ready at the same time.

If using a saucepan with a tiered steamer on top, potatoes (for instance) can be boiled directly in the water while other foods are steamed over the top. (You can't do this with an electric steamer, as you can't put any foods actually in the steaming water in the base.)

Many of the recipes in this book tell you how to cook accompaniments at the same time as the main course. If you want to cook a dessert too, you can either put it on to cook while you eat the main meal or, if it is to be served cold, steam, then cool and chill it before cooking the rest of the meal.

Reheating in a steamer

Steaming is the ideal way to reheat foods – everything from a shepherd's pie to bread rolls or a plated meal. The only important thing to remember is that food must be in a dish that fits in a steamer tier, or will sit snugly on top of a saucepan of simmering water.

Always make sure the food is piping hot throughout. The steaming time will depend on the quantity and density of the food – if it is piled up or tightly packed, the heat will take longer to penetrate.

To test if food is hot: Push a knife down through the centre of the reheated food. Hold for 5 seconds, then remove. The blade should feel burning hot. If not, steam for a little longer.

Reheating times

Different items take different lengths of time to reheat completely. The following list gives general guidance, but do always test with a knife before serving.

Family-sized made-up dish: Cover tightly with foil. Place in a steamer tier or on a dish over a pan of simmering water. Cover with a lid and steam for about 30 minutes or until piping hot throughout. The time will depend on the density of the food.

Plated meal: Put the meal on its plate over a pan of simmering water. Invert another plate over the top, or cover with a saucepan lid or foil. Make sure the food is covered completely. Steam for about 10 minutes or until piping hot throughout.

Bread rolls, flour tortillas, pancakes, etc: Wrap tightly in foil and place in a steamer tier, or place on a plate or in a shallow dish over a pan of simmering water. Cover with foil, then a lid. Steam for about 5 minutes or until piping hot.

Keeping food warm

Once reheated, foods can also be kept warm in the same way. Make sure the heat source is turned down as low as possible once the food is hot and make sure the water does not boil dry.

Safety first

Steam can cause severe scalding, so it is essential that you take great care when handling a steamer.

◇ Always use oven-gloves when lifting off the steamer tiers.

◇ Be careful when lifting off the steamer lid, unwrapping foil parcels or uncovering basins of steamed food. The steam inside will billow out and can easily burn your hands or face.

◇ Always use a kettle to top up boiling water in a saucepan during steaming. The spout will limit the possibility of splashing. Take extra care if you've let the pot boil completely dry – the hot water will splutter when you pour it into the container.

Basic food hygiene

A hygienic cook is a healthy cook – this applies whatever method of cooking you are using, so please bear the following in mind when you're preparing food for steaming.

◇ Always wash your hands first and don't lick your fingers, then touch food.
◇ Always wash and dry fresh produce before use.
◇ Don't keep tasting and stirring with the same spoon. Use a clean spoon every time you taste the food.
◇ Don't put raw and cooked meat on the same shelf in the fridge. Store raw meat on the bottom shelf, so it can't drip over other foods. Keep all perishable foods wrapped separately. Don't overfill the fridge or it will remain too warm.
◇ Never use a cloth to wipe down a chopping board you have been using for cutting up meat, for instance, then use the same one to wipe down your work surfaces – you will simply spread germs. Always wash your cloth well in hot, soapy water and, ideally, use an anti-bacterial kitchen cleaner on all surfaces too.
◇ Always transfer leftovers to a clean dish and cover with a lid, clingfilm (plastic wrap) or foil. Leave until completely cold, then store immediately in the fridge. Never put any warm food in the fridge.
◇ When reheating food, always make sure it is piping hot throughout, never just lukewarm.
◇ Don't re-freeze foods that have defrosted unless you cook them first. Never reheat previously cooked food more than once.

Your storecupboard

If you keep your storecupboard well stocked, you will always have the ingredients to hand to rustle up interesting meals at a moment's notice. This list includes most of the basics but you need only stock those items you would use regularly.

Packets and jars
◇ Baking powder
◇ Bicarbonate of soda (baking soda)
◇ Cocoa (unsweetened chocolate) powder
◇ Coffee, instant
◇ Cornflour (cornstarch)
◇ Couscous and/or bulgar (cracked wheat)
◇ Drinking (sweetened) chocolate powder – an instant chocolate drink powder, with added milk powder is good
◇ Flour – plain (all-purpose), self-raising (rising) and wholemeal
◇ Pasta – macaroni and/or other shapes, spaghetti, lasagne sheets, stuffed tortellini
◇ Rice – long-grain, risotto and pudding (round-grain)
◇ Sugar – caster (superfine), granulated, light and dark brown, icing (confectioners')

Herbs, flavourings and condiments
◇ Cranberry sauce
◇ Dried herbs – basil, chives, oregano, thyme, mint, sage, mixed herbs and bouquet garni sachets
◇ Dried onion flakes and dried red and green (bell) peppers – these are not vital but they're great for brightening up rice or pasta and they keep for ages
◇ Dried milk powder (non-fat dry milk)
◇ Garlic purée (paste) – use about 1 cm/½ in per garlic clove or to taste
◇ Honey, clear
◇ Horseradish sauce or cream
◇ Lemon juice – not vital but a bottle will keep in the fridge for ages and is better than vinegar in many recipes
◇ Marmalade
◇ Marmite or other yeast extract
◇ Mayonnaise
◇ Mustard – made English, Dijon and grainy
◇ Oil – sunflower, corn or groundnut (peanut) and olive, plus speciality ones like sesame and walnut for flavouring
◇ Pepper – peppercorns in a mill and ready-ground white
◇ Redcurrant jelly (clear conserve)
◇ Salt

◇ Spices – ground cinnamon, ginger and mace, cumin, turmeric, grated nutmeg, cayenne and/or chilli powder, paprika
◇ Stock cubes – vegetable, chicken, beef
◇ Table sauces – ketchup (catsup), brown, Worcestershire, soy and Tabasco, plus sweet chilli for dipping
◇ Tomato purée (paste)
◇ Vinegar – red or white wine or cider, balsamic, malt

Cans
◇ Baked beans
◇ Corned beef
◇ Custard, ready-made
◇ Fish – mackerel, pilchards, sardines, tuna
◇ Fruit – pineapple is very useful in cooking
◇ Ham
◇ Peas, carrots, green beans – useful for recipes and also for quick accompaniments
◇ Pulses – red kidney beans, butter (lima) beans, cannellini beans, etc.
◇ Rice pudding
◇ Soups – condensed mushroom, chicken and tomato are ideal for sauces
◇ Sweetcorn (corn)
◇ Tomatoes

Perishables
◇ Butter and/or margarine – I use a reduced-fat olive oil spread, suitable for cooking as well as spreading, plus hard block margarine for making pastry (paste)
◇ Eggs
◇ Bread loaves, rolls, pitta breads, naan, etc. – store in the freezer and take out when required
◇ Cheese – Cheddar and grated Parmesan, plus others as you need
◇ Yoghurt – plain for sauces and dressings and to eat with breakfast cereal or honey; fruit varieties for dessert
◇ Milk – cartons of milk can be frozen but they take ages to thaw and will need a good shake once defrosted
◇ Vegetables, frozen – mixed diced, plus peas and beans

Notes on the Recipes

◇ All ingredients are given in imperial, metric and American measures. Follow one set only in a recipe. American terms are given in brackets.

◇ All spoon measures are level: 1 tsp = 5 ml; 1 tbsp = 15 ml

◇ Eggs are medium unless otherwise stated.

◇ Always wash, peel, core and seed, if necessary, fresh produce before use.

◇ Seasoning and the use of strongly flavoured ingredients such as garlic and chillies are very much a matter of personal taste. Adjust to suit your own palate.

◇ Always use fresh herbs unless dried are specifically called for. If you wish to substitute dried for fresh, use only half the quantity or less, as they are very pungent. Frozen, chopped varieties have a better colour and flavour than the dried ones if fresh have been called for.

◇ All can and packet sizes are approximate as they vary from brand to brand. For example, if I call for a 400 g/14 oz/ large can of tomatoes and yours is a 397 g can, that's fine.

◇ I usually use sunflower or olive oil, but any good-quality oil, such as safflower or groundnut (peanut), will do just as well, if you prefer. I don't recommend the cheap ones just labelled 'vegetable oil' – their flavour is not good, and so they are particularly unsuitable for dressings.

◇ I have called for butter or margarine, cream and crème fraîche in many recipes. To reduce the fat content, use low-fat varieties, but do check that the spread you buy is suitable for cooking. Also take care with low-fat cream and crème fraîche, which may curdle if boiled, so should only be added at the end of cooking. To prevent curdling, blend a low-fat variety with 5 ml/1 tsp cornflour (cornstarch).

◇ Cooking times are approximate and should be used as a guide only. Always check food is piping hot and cooked through before serving.

Eggs and Cheese

You can 'steam-boil' and 'steam-bake' eggs to perfection and scrambled eggs cooked in a steamer turn out wonderfully creamy. They may take a little longer than when cooked conventionally but the results will be perfect every time. Cheese benefits from being steamed too – it melts beautifully instead of leaving you with tough, rubbery results. In this chapter, you'll find everything from simple starters and snacks to substantial main meals and desserts, all using eggs or cheese and, sometimes, both!

Steam-boiled eggs
SUITABLE FOR UP TO 8 EGGS

① Place the eggs in the special holder in the rice bowl of an electric steamer or in a bowl that will fit in or over a steamer. You can put them in an egg box to prevent them from rolling about but take care when removing them, the cardboard will be soggy and hot!

② Cover and steam for 8–10 minutes for soft-boiled; 15–20 minutes for hard-boiled (hard-cooked).

PREPARATION AND COOKING TIME: 10–20 MINUTES

Steamed scrambled eggs
SUITABLE FOR UP TO 8 EGGS

① Melt a knob of butter or margarine in a bowl over a pan of gently simmering water or the rice bowl of an electric steamer. Do not let the water touch the bowl.

② Whisk in the eggs and 15 ml/1 tbsp milk for each egg. Add seasoning to taste.

③ Cook, stirring all the time, until the eggs softly scramble but are still creamy. Do not overcook. Serve straight away.

PREPARATION AND COOKING TIME: 6–10 MINUTES

Steam-baked eggs
SUITABLE FOR UP TO 6 EGGS

① Lightly butter up to six ramekin dishes (custard cups), or as many as will fit in your steamer. Break an egg into each. Season lightly. Add a small spoonful of cream to each.

② Place in the steamer, cover with a lid and steam for 6–10 minutes or until the eggs are cooked to your liking.

PREPARATION AND COOKING TIME: 8–12 MINUTES

Steam-poached eggs
SUITABLE FOR UP TO 6 EGGS

① Put a tiny knob of butter in up to six ramekin dishes (custard cups). Place in a steamer to melt. Brush the butter round the dishes to grease, leaving a tiny pool in the base. Break an egg into each. Season lightly.

② Place in the steamer, cover with a lid and steam for 5–9 minutes or until cooked to your liking. Loosen the edge of each with a round-bladed knife and tip out on to hot buttered toast on warm plates.

PREPARATION AND COOKING TIME: 8–12 MINUTES

Chakchouka
SERVES 4

1 red (bell) pepper, halved and thinly sliced
1 green pepper, halved and thinly sliced
2 beefsteak tomatoes, skinned and chopped
1 garlic clove, crushed
15 ml/1 tbsp olive oil
15 ml/1 tbsp tomato purée (paste)
Salt and freshly ground black pepper
A good pinch of caster (superfine) sugar
4 eggs
To serve:
Flat breads, either bought or home-made (see page 138)

① Put the peppers, tomatoes, garlic, oil, tomato purée, a little salt and pepper and the sugar in a large shallow dish that will fit in or over a steamer or in the rice bowl of an electric steamer. Stir well. Cover with a lid and steam for 20 minutes, stirring once, until tender.

② Make four wells in the mixture and break an egg into each. Re-cover and steam for a further 6–10 minutes or until the eggs are cooked to your liking. Serve straight from the dish with flat breads.

PREPARATION AND COOKING TIME: 30–35 MINUTES

Creamy coddled eggs with smoked salmon croustades

SERVES 4

This makes a delicious lunch or supper dish. It will also make a starter for eight people.

2 ciabatta rolls, each cut into 4 slices lengthways
1 garlic clove, halved
30 ml/2 tbsp olive oil
15 g/½ oz/1 tbsp butter or margarine
8 eggs
120 ml/4 fl oz/½ cup double (heavy) cream
Salt and freshly ground black pepper
100 g/4 oz smoked salmon pieces
30 ml/2 tbsp chopped fresh parsley
Twists of lemon and sprigs of fresh parsley, for garnishing

① Rub the ciabatta slices all over with the garlic halves, then discard the garlic. Brush each slice with the olive oil. Place on a baking (cookie) sheet.

② Bake in a preheated oven at 220°C/425°F/gas mark 7 (fan oven 200°C) for about 12 minutes or until golden and crunchy. Remove from the oven.

③ Melt the butter or margarine in a fairly large bowl over a pan of simmering water or in the rice bowl of an electric steamer.

④ Add the eggs and beat until thoroughly blended, then beat in half the cream and add some salt and pepper. Cook, stirring all the time until beginning to scramble.

⑤ Separate the pieces of salmon and stir into the eggs with the parsley. Stir and cook for 1–2 minutes more until the eggs are creamy and just set. Stir in the remaining cream.

⑥ Pile on to the slices of ciabatta and garnish with twists of lemon and sprigs of parsley. Serve straight away.

PREPARATION AND COOKING TIME: ABOUT 20 MINUTES

Neapolitan-style ham and egg pots
SERVES 4

A little olive oil, for greasing
4 slices of Parma ham, finely chopped
2 canned plum tomatoes, chopped
8 fresh basil leaves, torn
4 eggs
60 ml/4 tbsp single (light) cream
Salt and freshly ground black pepper
To serve:
Focaccia bread

① Lightly oil four ramekin dishes (custard cups).

② Put some ham in the base of each and top with the tomato and the basil.

③ Break an egg into each dish. Spoon the cream over and season with salt and pepper.

④ Place in a steamer, cover with a lid and steam for 10–15 minutes or until the eggs are cooked to your liking. Serve hot with focaccia bread.

PREPARATION AND COOKING TIME: 15–20 MINUTES

Cheese soufflé
SERVES 4

Using the same recipe to make a single soufflé in a 15 cm/ 6 in dish will take about twice as long to cook.

120 ml/8 tbsp cheese spread
30 ml/2 tbsp milk
30 ml/2 tbsp plain (all-purpose) flour
1.5 ml/¼ tsp made English mustard
Salt and freshly ground black pepper
2 eggs, separated
45 ml/3 tbsp crushed cornflakes

① Put the cheese spread, milk, flour and mustard in a bowl and season with a little salt and pepper. Stir in the egg yolks and beat until smooth.

② Whisk the egg whites until stiff and fold into the mixture with a metal spoon.

③ Grease four ramekin dishes (custard cups). Spoon the mixture into the dishes and sprinkle with the cornflakes.

④ Place in a steamer, cover with a lid and steam for 10 minutes until risen and set. Serve immediately.

PREPARATION AND COOKING TIME: 15 MINUTES

Melting cheese, mushroom and chutney rolls
SERVES 4

4 soft round rolls
200 g/7 oz/1 small can of creamed mushrooms
5 ml/1 tsp dried oregano
20 ml/4 tsp tomato chutney
50 g/2 oz/½ cup Mozzarella cheese, grated
50 g/2 oz/½ cup Cheddar cheese, grated
To serve:
A crisp salad

① Cut the top off each roll and pull out most of the soft bread, leaving a thick wall all round.

② Spoon the mushrooms into the rolls and sprinkle with the oregano. Top each with a spoonful of chutney.

③ Mix the cheeses together and pack into the rolls. Cover with the 'lids'. Wrap each one in foil.

④ Transfer to a steamer, cover with a lid and steam for 10 minutes until the cheese has melted.

⑤ Unwrap and serve straight away with a crisp salad.

PREPARATION AND COOKING TIME: 15 MINUTES

Cheddar and gruyère fondue with crudités

SERVES 4

You can, of course, serve this fondue with chunks of French bread to dip in instead of the vegetable sticks.

---

100 g/4 oz/1 cup Cheddar cheese, grated
100 g/4 oz/1 cup Gruyère (Swiss) cheese, grated
10 ml/2 tsp cornflour (cornstarch)
90 ml/6 tbsp fruity dry white wine, such as Chardonnay
15 ml/1 tbsp kirsch or vodka
60 ml/4 tbsp crème fraîche
A pinch of cayenne
Freshly ground black pepper
1 large carrot, cut into matchsticks
2 celery sticks, cut into matchsticks
5 cm/2 in piece of cucumber, cut into matchsticks
1 red (bell) pepper, halved and cut into strips

---

① Put the cheeses in a bowl over a pan of simmering water, or in a double saucepan or the rice bowl of an electric steamer, and stir in the cornflour. Add the wine and kirsch or vodka.

② Steam for about 10 minutes, stirring until the mixture is melted and creamy.

③ Stir in the crème fraîche and season the fondue with the cayenne and black pepper to taste.

④ Arrange the vegetables on four plates. Spoon the fondue into warmed individual pots, place on the plates with the crudités and serve straight away.

PREPARATION AND COOKING TIME: 25 MINUTES

Blue cheese and celery cocottes

SERVES 4

This is delicious as a starter or as a light lunch, served with crusty bread and a salad.

2 tender young celery sticks, very finely chopped
50 g/2 oz/1 cup fresh white breadcrumbs
50 g/2 oz/^{1}/$_2$ cup blue cheese, crumbled
2 eggs, separated
75 ml/5 tbsp crème fraîche
75–90 ml/5–6 tbsp milk
30 ml/2 tbsp snipped fresh chives
Salt and freshly ground black pepper
15 ml/1 tbsp tomato ketchup (catsup)
10 ml/2 tsp tomato purée (paste)
2.5 ml/^{1}/$_2$ tsp Worcestershire sauce
A small handful of whole fresh chive stalks, for garnishing

① Grease four ramekin dishes (custard cups) and line the bases with circles of greased greaseproof (waxed) paper.

② Mix the celery with the breadcrumbs and cheese. Beat the egg yolks with 60 ml/4 tbsp of the crème fraîche and 60 ml/4 tbsp of the milk and mix in. Stir in the snipped chives and some salt and pepper.

③ Whisk the egg whites until stiff and fold in with a metal spoon. Turn into the ramekin dishes. Place in a steamer, cover with a lid and steam for 20 minutes until set.

④ Meanwhile, mix the remaining crème fraîche with the tomato ketchup, purée and Worcestershire sauce and add enough of the remaining milk to give a thick pouring consistency.

⑤ Loosen the edges of the cocottes with a round-bladed knife. Turn out on to warm plates and remove the circles of paper. Spoon a little sauce round the bases of the cocottes.

⑥ Arrange a few chive stalks in a criss-cross pattern on top of the cocottes and serve straight away.

PREPARATION AND COOKING TIME: 30 MINUTES

Nutty camembert with cranberry sauce
SERVES 4

8 individual wedges of Camembert, chilled
1 large egg, beaten
100 g/4 oz/1 cup toasted chopped mixed nuts
60 ml/4 tbsp cranberry sauce
Mixed lettuce leaves and French dressing, for garnishing
To serve:
Hot rolls

① Dip the cheese wedges in the egg, then the nuts. Repeat to cover well, pressing the nuts on firmly.

② Place on lightly oiled foil in a steamer. Cover with a lid and steam for 5 minutes.

③ Transfer to individual plates. Spoon cranberry sauce to one side of each and garnish with salad leaves and a drizzle of French dressing. Serve straight away with hot rolls.

PREPARATION AND COOKING TIME: 10 MINUTES

Egg custard
SERVES 4

2 eggs
15 ml/1 tbsp caster (superfine) sugar
450 ml/³/₄ pt/2 cups milk
A little grated nutmeg

① Beat the eggs and sugar together in a serving dish that will fit in or over your steamer.

② Warm the milk and pour over, whisking all the time.

③ Sprinkle with nutmeg and transfer to the steamer. Cover with a lid and steam for 1¼ hours until set.

④ Serve warm or cold.

PREPARATION AND COOKING TIME: 1 HOUR 20 MINUTES

Fluffy tíramísu
SERVES 6–8

A traditional tiramisu has raw egg yolks in it. This version gently cooks the mixture and is much lighter.

250 g/9 oz/generous 1 cup Mascarpone cheese
2 eggs, separated
50 g/2 oz/¼ cup caster (superfine) sugar
10 ml/2 tsp instant coffee granules or powder
60 ml/4 tbsp amaretto liqueur or brandy
8 trifle sponges, halved lengthways
150 ml/¼ pt/⅔ cup double (heavy) cream, whipped
30 ml/2 tbsp finely grated chocolate

① Beat the cheese with the egg yolks and sugar.

② Dissolve 5 ml/1 tsp of the coffee in 15 ml/1 tbsp hot water, then stir into the mixture.

③ Whisk the egg whites until stiff and fold into the mixture with a metal spoon.

④ Dissolve the remaining coffee in 120 ml/4 fl oz/½ cup water and add the liqueur.

⑤ Dip the halved sponges in the coffee and liqueur mixture and lay half in the base of a 20 cm/8 in soufflé dish.

⑥ Spread half the cheese mixture over, then top with the remaining dipped sponges and finally the remaining cheese mixture.

⑦ Cover the dish with well-greased foil with a pleat in the centre to allow for rising. Twist and fold under the rim to secure. Transfer to a steamer, cover with a lid and steam for 30 minutes.

⑧ Remove the foil, leave to cool, then chill.

⑨ Spread the top with whipped cream, then cover with the grated chocolate before serving.

PREPARATION AND COOKING TIME: 45 MINUTES PLUS CHILLING

Zabaglione
SERVES 4

This Italian dessert is traditionally made with egg yolks, but I find this whole-egg version works just as well.

2 eggs
25 g/1 oz/2 tbsp caster (superfine) sugar
45 ml/3 tbsp Marsala or sweet or medium-dry sherry
To serve:
Sponge (lady) fingers

① Put the eggs in a large bowl with the sugar and Marsala or sherry. Stand the bowl over a pan of gently simmering water.

② Whisk with a balloon or electric whisk until thick, creamy and voluminous.

③ Spoon into wine goblets and serve with a sponge finger tucked down the side of each glass.

PREPARATION AND COOKING TIME: 7 MINUTES

Fruit zabaglione
Put a few fresh raspberries, small strawberries or sliced peaches or nectarines in the base of each glass before adding the Zabaglione. Use a complementary fruit liqueur instead of the Marsala or sherry, if liked.

Lemon sabayon
SERVES 4–6

4 egg yolks
40 g/1½ oz/3 tbsp caster (superfine) sugar
Finely grated rind and juice of ½ large lemon
300 ml/½ pt/1¼ cups medium-dry or sweet white wine
30 ml/2 tbsp brandy
4–6 ratafia biscuits (cookies)

① Put the egg yolks, sugar, lemon rind and juice and half the wine in a large bowl. Stand the bowl over a pan of gently simmering water and whisk with a balloon or electric whisk until thick and frothy.

② Whisk in the remaining wine and the brandy until really thick, creamy and voluminous.

③ Put a ratafia in the base of each wine goblet. Spoon the sabayon over and serve straight away.

PREPARATION AND COOKING TIME: 15 MINUTES

Crème brûlée with blueberries
SERVES 4–6

If you prefer, you can heat the sugar slowly in a saucepan until it melts and caramelises to a rich golden brown, then simply pour it over the top of the set cream. You will get a more even, shiny finish rather than the traditional 'tortoiseshell' appearance.

2 large eggs
100 g/4 oz/¹/₂ cup caster (superfine) sugar
450 ml/³/₄ pt/2 cups double (heavy) cream
4 ml/³/₄ tsp vanilla essence (extract)
100 g/4 oz blueberries

① Whisk the eggs with 30 ml/2 tbsp of the sugar and the cream until well blended.

② Put the fruit in the base of a 15 cm/6 in soufflé dish. Pour the cream mixture over. Place in a steamer, cover with a lid and steam for 1 hour or until set.

③ Leave to cool, then chill.

④ Sprinkle with the remaining sugar to cover the top completely. Either caramelise with a blow torch or place the dishes under a preheated grill until the sugar melts and caramelises. Cool again and chill until ready to serve.

PREPARATION AND COOKING TIME: 1 HOUR 10 MINUTES PLUS CHILLING

Chocolate marbled cheesecake

SERVES 8–10

175 g/6 oz/1½ cups chocolate digestive biscuits (graham crackers), crushed

50 g/2 oz/¼ cup butter, melted

400 g/14 oz/scant 2 cups medium-fat soft cheese

175 g/6 oz/¾ cup caster (superfine) sugar

1 large egg

2.5 ml/½ tsp vanilla essence (extract)

100 g/4 oz/1 cup plain (semi-sweet) chocolate, broken into pieces

150 ml/¼ pt/⅔ cup crème fraîche

A little grated nutmeg

① Mix the crushed biscuits with the butter and press into the base of a greased, loose-bottomed 18 cm/7 in cake tin (pan).

② Beat the cheese with the sugar, egg and vanilla essence.

③ Melt the chocolate in a fairly large bowl over a pan of simmering water.

④ Stir half the cheese mixture into the melted chocolate, then tip this into the white cheese mixture and gently stir just enough to give a marbled effect. Do not mix completely.

⑤ Turn into the cake tin and smooth the surface. Cover the tin with foil, place in a steamer, cover with a lid and steam for 2 hours. Remove the foil, leave to cool, then chill.

⑥ Spread the crème fraîche over the surface and dust with a little grated nutmeg.

PREPARATION AND COOKING TIME: 2¼ HOURS PLUS CHILLING

Hazelnut moulds with raspberry coulis

SERVES 6

You can stew the raspberries first in a saucepan, if you prefer.

2 whole eggs
2 egg yolks
50 g/2 oz/¼ cup soft light brown sugar
600 ml/1 pt/2½ cups double (heavy) cream
100 g/4 oz/1 cup ground hazelnuts (filberts)
A few drops of vanilla essence (extract)
350 g/12 oz fresh or thawed frozen raspberries
25 g/1 oz/3 tbsp icing (confectioners') sugar
A squeeze of lemon juice
A few tiny sprigs of fresh mint (optional)

① Lightly oil six ramekin dishes (custard cups) and line the base of each with a circle of greased greaseproof (waxed) paper.

② Whisk the eggs, yolks, sugar and cream together with the nuts. Spoon into the ramekin dishes.

③ Place in a steamer, cover with a lid and steam for 40 minutes until set. Leave to cool, then chill.

④ Meanwhile, reserve 18 raspberries for decoration and put the remainder with the icing sugar in a bowl that will fit in a steamer tier over the ramekins or in the rice bowl of an electric steamer. Steam for 10 minutes until the juices run. Purée in a blender or food processor and pass through a sieve (strainer) into a bowl to remove the seeds. Sharpen the purée with lemon juice to taste, then leave to cool.

⑤ Loosen the edges of the hazelnut creams and tip out on to six dessert plates. Remove the paper. Drizzle the raspberry coulis around. Decorate each cream with a cluster of three raspberries and add a tiny sprig of mint, if liked.

PREPARATION AND COOKING TIME: 1 HOUR PLUS CHILLING

Seafood

*T*he big danger when cooking seafood of any kind is overdoing it – fish can become dry and unappetising very quickly. Steaming prevents this, keeping it moist and succulent.

In this chapter you'll find everything from impressive starters for a dinner party to delicious main courses suitable for both everyday and special occasions. We are all encouraged to eat more fish because they contain omega-3 fatty acids, which can help prevent heart disease. They are also natural sources of vitamins A and D and iodine – all essential for good health.

Steaming seafood

There are several ways of steaming fillets and whole fish. The simplest way is simply to lay the fish, just as it is, on a lightly buttered plate or piece of foil. It may also be steamed in liquid such as milk, stock or wine; or *en papillote,* a French culinary term, meaning 'in a paper'. The fish is wrapped in foil or greaseproof (waxed) paper parcels with herbs, spices and a little moistening agent such as butter, wine or citrus juice. Remember, if you add other ingredients such as vegetables to the parcels, the cooking time will be slightly longer.

Shellfish can be cooked directly in a steamer tier, or in a very little liquid.

Cooking times for seafood

Fillets: 5–15 minutes, depending on quantity and thickness
Whole fish and thick steaks: 15–30 minutes, depending on size
Molluscs in shells and other shellfish: 5–10 minutes, depending on quantity

To tell whether fish is cooked

Fillets and steaks: These should look opaque and the flakes (called 'myotomes') should separate easily with the point of a knife.

Whole unstuffed fish: Check the body cavity – the flesh should look opaque.

Whole stuffed fish: The flesh should feel firm to the touch.

Molluscs, e.g. mussels: The shells should open when they are cooked. Discard any that remain closed.

Raw prawns (shrimp), langoustines, etc: These turn from blue-grey to pink. Cook until they just turn colour completely. The shell of unpeeled shellfish will change colour very quickly, so make sure the underside, where the legs are, has also turned pink.

Scallops: These turn opaque when cooked. When pressed, they should feel just firm but slightly spongy, not hard.

Red mullet parcels with fresh basil, olives and sun-dried tomatoes

SERVES 4

If you have a tiered steamer, cook the potatoes in the bottom tier for 10–15 minutes before adding the second tier with the fish parcels. Alternatively, cook the potatoes in a pan of boiling, salted water, with a single steamer fitted over the top, containing the fish, for the fish cooking time.

15 g/½ oz/1 tbsp butter or margarine
4 courgettes (zucchini), thinly sliced
4 red mullet fillets, about 175 g/6 oz each
30 ml/2 tbsp stoned (pitted) black olives, sliced
4 sun-dried tomatoes in oil, drained and very finely sliced
12 fresh basil leaves, torn
Salt and freshly ground black pepper
15 ml/1 tbsp sun-dried tomato oil (from the jar)
15 ml/1 tbsp lemon juice
To serve:
New potatoes and a green salad

① Cut four large squares of foil or double-thickness greaseproof (waxed) paper. Fold in halves, then open out. Spread the butter or margarine over half the paper or foil.

② Arrange the sliced courgettes over the butter or margarine and top with the fish. Scatter the olives, sun-dried tomatoes and basil over and season with salt and pepper.

③ Whisk the tomato oil and lemon juice together and sprinkle over the fish.

④ Fold the greaseproof paper or foil over the top, and twist and fold securely all round to fasten tightly. Place in a steamer, cover with a lid and steam for 20 minutes.

⑥ Transfer the parcels to warm plates and open at the table so guests get the full aroma of the fragrant contents. Serve with new potatoes and a green salad.

PREPARATION AND COOKING TIME: 30 MINUTES

Mussels in wine with fennel and shallots
SERVES 4

If you are using an electric steamer for this, use the rice bowl at its lowest position in the machine.

1.8 kg/4 lb fresh mussels in their shells, scrubbed and
   beards removed
1 head of fennel
15 g/½ oz/1 tbsp butter or margarine
4 shallots, finely chopped
1 carrot, finely chopped
250 ml/8 fl oz/1 cup dry white wine
120 ml/4 fl oz/½ cup water
Freshly ground black pepper
15 ml/1 tbsp cornflour (cornstarch)
15 ml/1 tbsp brandy
150 ml/¼ pt/⅔ cup crème fraîche
To serve:
French bread and a green salad

① Discard any mussels that are broken or open and those that don't close when sharply tapped.

② Chop the fennel, reserving the feathery fronds for garnish. Heat the butter or margarine in a large saucepan. Add the shallots, fennel and carrot and fry (sauté), stirring, for 2 minutes until softened but not browned.

③ Stir in the wine and water and add a good grinding of pepper. Tip in the mussels. Cover with a tight-fitting lid and steam for 10 minutes or until the mussels open. Using a draining spoon, transfer the mussels to a large warm serving bowl, discarding any that have not opened.

④ Blend the cornflour with the brandy and stir into the cooking liquid. Bring to the boil, stirring, then stir in the crème fraîche. Taste and re-season if necessary. Pile the mussels into warm bowls. Pour the cooking liquid over, sprinkle with the reserved chopped fennel fronds and serve with lots of French bread and a green salad.

PREPARATION AND COOKING TIME: ABOUT 40 MINUTES

Trout fillets in vermouth with a saffron and prawn sauce

SERVES 4

4 trout fillets, about 175 g/6 oz each
Salt and freshly ground black pepper
150 ml/¼ pt/⅔ cup dry vermouth
150 ml/¼ pt/⅔ cup fish or chicken stock, made with
 ½ stock cube
1 bay leaf
2.5 ml/½ tsp saffron powder
10 ml/2 tsp cornflour (cornstarch)
10 ml/2 tsp water
150 ml/¼ pt/⅔ cup double (heavy) cream
100 g/4 oz cooked peeled prawns (shrimp)
A few nasturtium flowers or whole fresh chive stalks, for
 garnishing
To serve:
Creamed potatoes and mangetout (snow peas)

① Wipe the fish and lay them in a shallow heatproof dish that will fit in or over a steamer or in the rice bowl of an electric steamer. Season with a little salt and pepper and pour on half the vermouth and stock. Add the bay leaf. Cover with a lid or foil and steam for 10–15 minutes.

② Carefully pour off the liquid into a saucepan and add the remaining vermouth and stock and the saffron. Cover the fish and keep warm.

③ Boil the cooking liquid mixture rapidly for 5 minutes until reduced by half. Blend the cornflour with the water and stir in. Bring to the boil and cook for 1 minute, stirring. Stir in the cream and prawns and heat through. Taste and re-season if necessary.

④ Transfer the trout to warm plates. Spoon the sauce over. Garnish with nasturtium flowers or chives and serve with creamed potatoes and mangetout.

PREPARATION AND COOKING TIME: ABOUT 25 MINUTES

Mackerel with madras mustard rub
SERVES 4

If you like a sharp, spicy taste, put lime pickle instead of mango chutney inside the fish.

4 even-sized mackerel, cleaned
15 ml/1 tbsp madras curry powder
15 ml/1 tbsp mustard powder
5 ml/1 tsp ground cumin
5 ml/1 tsp caster (superfine) sugar
2.5 ml/½ tsp salt
A good grinding of black pepper
20 ml/4 tsp mango chutney
Sprigs of fresh coriander (cilantro) and wedges of lemon, for garnishing
To serve:
Mango chutney, basmati rice and a crisp salad

① Rinse the fish inside and out and wipe dry with kitchen paper (paper towels). Make several slashes on each side of the fish. Remove the heads. Place each fish on a large square of oiled foil.

② Mix together all the ingredients except the chutney and rub all over the mackerel, pressing into the slits and inside the body. Put a spoonful of chutney in each body cavity.

③ Wrap up the fish in the foil, folding the ends securely to seal. Place in the fridge to marinate for 1–4 hours.

④ Place in one or two tiers over a steamer, cover with a lid and steam for 20 minutes. If using two tiers, switch their positions halfway through cooking.

⑤ Unwrap and transfer the fish to warm plates. Garnish with sprigs of coriander and wedges of lemon and serve with mango chutney, rice and a crisp salad.

PREPARATION AND COOKING TIME: 25 MINUTES PLUS MARINATING

Plaice on garlic croûtes with egg and tarragon sauce
SERVES 4

This also makes a delicious starter for eight people – without the serving suggestions of course! If you aren't keen on tarragon, use parsley instead.

4 whole plaice fillets, cut into halves and skinned
10 ml/2 tsp lemon juice
Salt and freshly ground black pepper
65 g/2¹/₂ oz/scant ¹/₃ cup butter or margarine
2 eggs
30 ml/2 tbsp sunflower oil
1 garlic clove, quartered
8 slices of French bread
15 g/¹/₂ oz/2 tbsp plain (all-purpose) flour
150 ml/¹/₄ pt/²/₃ cup milk
60 ml/4 tbsp single (light) cream
15 ml/1 tbsp chopped fresh tarragon
To serve:
Wild rice mix and peas

① If using a saucepan, fill with boiling water. Sprinkle the fish with the lemon juice and some salt and pepper. Roll up and arrange either in a large, open dish that will sit on top of the saucepan or in the rice bowl of an electric steamer, well-greased with a little of the butter or margarine.

② Add the eggs to the pan of water or to a steamer tier of the electric steamer. Put the plate or bowl of fish on top. Cover with a lid or foil and steam for 15–20 minutes or until cooked through.

③ Meanwhile, heat all but 15 g/¹/₂ oz/1 tbsp of the butter or margarine with the oil in a large frying pan (skillet). Add the garlic and fry (sauté) for 1 minute. Add the bread and fry on both sides until golden. Drain on kitchen paper (paper towels) and discard the garlic. Keep warm.

④ When the fish and eggs are cooked, remove the eggs, plunge into boiling water, then shell and chop finely. Melt the remaining butter or margarine in a small saucepan. Stir in the flour and cook for 1 minute. Remove from the heat, then gradually stir in the milk. Bring to the boil and cook for 2 minutes, stirring. Stir in the fish cooking liquid and the cream. Reserve a little chopped egg and tarragon, add the remainder to the sauce. Season and heat through.

⑤ Put the croûtes on warm plates and top with the fish rolls. Spoon over a little sauce and garnish with the remaining egg and tarragon. Serve hot with wild rice and peas.

PREPARATION AND COOKING TIME: ABOUT 30 MINUTES

Tiger prawns in chilli and chive butter
SERVES 4

100 g/4 oz/½ cup butter or margarine
Finely grated rind and juice of ½ small lemon
1 green chilli, seeded and finely chopped
24 raw tiger prawns (jumbo shrimp), peeled but tails left on
Salt and freshly ground black pepper.
30 ml/2 tbsp snipped fresh chives
Wedges of lemon and whole chive stalks, for garnishing
To serve:
French bread

① Put the butter or margarine in a shallow bowl that will fit in or over a steamer or in the rice bowl of an electric steamer. Add the lemon rind, juice and chilli and steam for 1 minute.

② Add the prawns and baste in the melted fat. Season lightly with salt and add lots of pepper.

③ Cover with a lid and steam for 5 minutes until the prawns are pink. Stir in the snipped chives. Taste and re-season.

④ Spoon onto individual warm plates and garnish with wedges of lemon and a few chive stalks. Serve with French bread.

PREPARATION AND COOKING TIME: 10 MINUTES

Crab-stuffed cucumber with dressed crab hollandaise

SERVES 4

---

1 large cucumber
Salt and freshly ground black pepper
225 g/8 oz/1 medium can of chopped tomatoes
170 g/6 oz/1 small can of white crabmeat
50 g/2 oz/1 cup fresh white breadcrumbs
5 ml/1 tsp anchovy essence (extract)
A few drops of Tabasco sauce
2 eggs
15 ml/1 tbsp lemon juice
100 g/4 oz/½ cup butter or margarine, cut into small pieces
40 g/1½ oz/1 very small can of dressed crab
5 ml/1 tsp tomato ketchup (catsup)
15 ml/1 tbsp chopped fresh coriander (cilantro), for garnishing
To serve:
Crusty bread and a mixed salad

---

① Cut the cucumber in half widthways, then cut each half lengthways. Scoop out the seeds to form 'boats'. Sprinkle with salt and leave to stand for 15 minutes. Rinse thoroughly and pat dry with kitchen paper (paper towels).

② Drain the can of tomatoes. Mix with the crab, breadcrumbs, anchovy essence, a few drops of Tabasco sauce and salt and pepper to taste. Pack into the cucumber.

③ Place in a shallow dish that will fit in or over a steamer. Cover with a lid or foil and steam for 30 minutes.

④ Meanwhile, whisk the eggs in a bowl that will fit over the steamer tier or in the rice bowl of an electric steamer. Whisk in the lemon juice. Gradually whisk in the butter or margarine, a few pieces at a time, whisking well after each addition, until thick and creamy. Whisk in the dressed crab and tomato ketchup. Season to taste.

⑤ Transfer the stuffed cucumber to warm plates. Spoon the sauce over and garnish with chopped coriander before serving with crusty bread and a mixed salad.

PREPARATION AND COOKING TIME: 45 MINUTES

Cod with melted cheese and tomatoes
SERVES 4

If cooking the potatoes too, put them in the bottom tier of a steamer and steam for 30 minutes before adding the fish in another tier.

---

4 pieces of thick cod fillet, about 175 g/6 oz each
Salt and freshly ground black pepper
5 ml/1 tsp dried oregano
3 tomatoes, thickly sliced
100 g/4 oz/1 cup Cheddar cheese, grated
30 ml/2 tbsp crushed cornflakes
15 ml/1 tbsp chopped fresh parsley
Scalloped Potatoes (see page 97) and broccoli, to serve

---

① Wipe the fish and place on foil or in a shallow dish that will fit in or over a steamer.

② Season lightly, then sprinkle with the oregano. Top with the tomato slices and finally the cheese.

③ Cover with a lid or foil and steam for 15–20 minutes until cooked through and the cheese has melted.

④ Transfer to warm plates. Sprinkle with the cornflakes and parsley and serve with Scalloped Potatoes and broccoli.

PREPARATION AND COOKING TIME: 20–25 MINUTES

Squid in olive oil, garlic and parsley
SERVES 4

1 onion, finely chopped
2 garlic cloves, crushed
90 ml/6 tbsp olive oil
25 g/1 oz/2 tbsp unsalted (sweet) butter
8 squid tubes, sliced into rings and tentacles cut into
   pieces
Salt and freshly ground black pepper
5 ml/1 tsp lemon juice
30 ml/2 tbsp chopped fresh parsley
Wedges of lemon and sprigs of fresh parsley,
   for garnishing
To serve:
French bread

① Put the onion and garlic with the oil and butter in a dish over a pan of simmering water or in the rice bowl of an electric steamer. Cover with a lid or foil and steam for 5 minutes.

② Add the squid to the onion and garlic with some salt and pepper and the lemon juice. Cover and steam for 15 minutes.

③ Taste and re-season, if necessary, then stir in the parsley. Spoon the squid and all the lovely juices into warm bowls. Garnish with each with a wedge of lemon and a sprig of parsley and serve with French bread.

PREPARATION AND COOKING TIME: 25 MINUTES

Smoked haddock with wilted spinach and steam-poached eggs
SERVES 4

25 g/1 oz/2 tbsp butter or margarine
250 g/9 oz young spinach leaves, well-washed and dried
Salt and freshly ground black pepper
4 smoked haddock fillets, about 175 g/6 oz each, skinned
60 ml/4 tbsp milk
4 eggs
A little cayenne (optional)
To serve:
Hot buttered toast

① Lightly grease four large squares of foil or double-thickness greaseproof (waxed) paper with a little of the butter or margarine. Pile the spinach in the centre of each and sprinkle very lightly with salt.

② Rinse the fish, pat dry on kitchen paper (paper towels) and lay one on the top of each pile of spinach.

③ Add 15 ml/1 tbsp milk to each and add a good grinding of pepper. Wrap in the foil or greaseproof paper, sealing the ends tightly. Arrange in a steamer, so that there is room for steam to circulate. Steam for 15 minutes.

④ Grease four ramekin dishes (custard cups) thoroughly with the remaining butter or margarine. Break in the eggs. Place in the steamer above the fish, preferably in a second tier, and steam for 6–10 minutes until cooked to your liking.

⑤ Carefully open the parcels and slide the fish and spinach on to warm plates, letting the juices run out. Gently loosen each egg with a round-bladed knife and tip out on to the fish. Sprinkle with a little cayenne, if liked. Serve with hot buttered toast.

PREPARATION AND COOKING TIME: 25 MINUTES

Salmon steaks with citrus and fragrant herbs

SERVES 4

You can use ready-made mayonnaise or try my delicious recipe for cooked mayonnaise on page 147.

A little butter or margarine, for greasing
4 pieces of salmon fillet, about 175 g/6 oz each, skinned
1 lime
1 orange
Salt and freshly ground black pepper
4 sprigs of fresh rosemary
4 sprigs of fresh thyme
To serve:
Mayonnaise, new potatoes, baby corn cobs and
    mangetout (snow peas)

① Cut four large squares of foil or double-thickness greaseproof (waxed) paper and lightly grease with butter or margarine. Lay a piece of fish in the centre of each.

② Cut off four thin slices from the lime and the orange and reserve for garnish. Finely grate the rind of the remaining lime and orange and squeeze the juice.

③ Spoon over each piece of fish and sprinkle with the sugar and a little salt and pepper. Arrange the lime and orange slices on top and then lay a sprig each of rosemary and thyme on each fillet. Wrap securely in the foil or paper, folding the ends tightly to seal.

④ Place in a steamer, cover with a lid and steam for 15–20 minutes (the time will depend on the thickness of the fish).

⑤ Transfer the parcels to warm plates. Serve with mayonnaise, new potatoes, baby corn cobs and mangetout.

PREPARATION AND COOKING TIME: 20–25 MINUTES

Leicestershire fish pie
SERVES 4

700 g/1½ lb potatoes, peeled and cut into small chunks
Salt and freshly ground black pepper
450 g/1 lb white fish fillet, skinned
1 bay leaf
375 ml/6 fl oz /1½ cups milk
2 eggs
20 g/¾ oz/3 tbsp plain (all-purpose) flour
25 g/1 oz/2 tbsp butter or margarine
30 ml/2 tbsp chopped fresh parsley
50 g/2 oz/½ cup Red Leicester cheese, grated
To serve:
Peas

① Put the potato pieces in a steamer and season with salt or place in salted water in a saucepan. Cover and steam or boil for 5 minutes.

② Meanwhile, put the fish in a large piece of foil with the bay leaf and a little seasoning. Pour on 150 ml/¼ pt/⅔ cup of the milk. Wrap up securely and place in the steamer or in a steamer container on top of the saucepan. Add the eggs. Cover and steam for 15 minutes until the fish and potatoes are tender and the eggs hard-boiled (hard-cooked).

③ Blend the flour with 150 ml/¼ pt/⅔ cup of the remaining milk in a saucepan. Add half the butter or margarine. Carefully pour in the fish cooking milk from the parcel and return the parcel to the steamer to keep warm over a low heat.

④ Bring to the boil, stirring all the time, and cook for 2 minutes. Season, then stir in the parsley. Flake the fish and add. Shell the eggs, cut into chunks and add. Turn the mixture into a flameproof serving dish. Mash the potatoes with the remaining milk and butter or margarine. Pile on top and cover with the cheese.

⑥ Brown under a preheated grill (broiler). Serve with peas.

PREPARATION AND COOKING TIME: 40 MINUTES

Hake with asparagus and green hollandaise

SERVES 4

You can use any meaty white fish for this recipe.

1 bunch of watercress
4 hake steaks, about 175 g/6 oz each
5 ml/1 tsp dried mixed herbs
Salt and freshly ground black pepper
15 g/½ oz/1 tbsp butter or margarine
225 g/8 oz short asparagus spears, trimmed
1 quantity of Hollandaise sauce (see page 148)
30 ml/2 tbsp chopped fresh parsley
To serve:
New potatoes and baby carrots

① Reserve a few sprigs of watercress for garnishing, then finely chop the remainder.

② Put the fish on foil in a steamer and sprinkle with the herbs, a little salt and pepper and dot with the butter or margarine. Arrange the asparagus around and sprinkle lightly with salt.

③ Cover with a lid and steam for 10 minutes.

④ Meanwhile, make the Hollandaise sauce in the rice bowl, if using an electric steamer, or in a bowl over a pan of simmering water.

⑤ Stir in the chopped watercress and parsley.

⑥ Transfer the asparagus to warm plates and arrange neatly in the centre. Top with the hake and spoon the green sauce over. Garnish each portion with a sprig of watercress and serve with new potatoes and baby carrots.

PREPARATION AND COOKING TIME: ABOUT 15 MINUTES

Meat and Poultry

Steamed meat and poultry remain moist, tender and succulent: even cuts that you might normally fry (sauté) or grill (broil) can be given the steam treatment and the results will be meltingly juicy. Meat is also more digestible steamed than when cooked in lots of fat, as the fibres are gently softened in the moist heat.

Obviously, when steaming meat and poultry, you can't crisp and brown the outside as you can when grilling, roasting or frying. To achieve this, brown the meat first in a frying pan (skillet) or flash the cooked meat under a hot grill (broiler) at the end. Colour can also be added with marinades, sauces and toppings.

To prepare steamed vegetables to serve with any of the following recipes, simply add them to a steamer tier above the meat for the appropriate cooking time (see pages 88–92).

Cooking times for steaming meat and poultry

Obviously, cooking times for casseroles will vary according to the quantity of food they contain. For chops, chicken breasts, etc., thickness is the crucial factor. Always arrange them in a single layer, allowing room for the steam to circulate.

The following are offered as a guide only.

Chicken breasts between two plates or wrapped in foil: 20 minutes

Chops or steaks up to 1 cm/½ in thick: 20 minutes

Chops or steaks, thicker than the above: 30 minutes. For rare beef steaks, cook for 10–15 minutes only, depending on thickness

Chicken portions: 40–45 minutes

Escalopes (beaten steaks) and thin fillets: 10 minutes

Pork and egg terrine
SERVES 4–6

225 g/8 oz pig's liver, trimmed
1 small onion
450 g/1 lb minced (ground) pork
225 g/8 oz lean pork sausagemeat
30 ml/2 tbsp chopped fresh parsley
15 ml/1 tbsp chopped fresh sage
50 g/2 oz/1 cup fresh white breadcrumbs
Salt and freshly ground black pepper
1 egg, beaten
4 large green cabbage leaves, stalks removed
3 hard-boiled (hard-cooked) eggs, shelled
A few cherry tomatoes, quartered
To serve:
A mixed salad, mustard and crusty bread

① Mince or finely chop the liver and onion. Mix with the minced pork, sausagemeat, herbs, breadcrumbs and some salt and pepper. Season well and mix with the beaten egg, to bind.

② Use the cabbage leaves to line a greased 900 g/ 2 lb loaf tin (pan), leaving the edges of the leaves overhanging the tin. Spoon half the meat mixture in the tin and press down well. Put a line of hard-boiled eggs down the centre, then fill with the remaining meat mixture. Press down again.

③ Fold the cabbage leaves over the top, then cover with greased greaseproof (waxed) paper or foil, twisting and folding under the rim to secure. Place in a steamer or a bain marie (see page 7), cover and steam for 2 hours.

④ Remove the paper or foil, cover with fresh paper or foil and weigh down with heavy weights or cans of food. Leave until cold, then chill for several hours or overnight.

⑤ Turn out, garnish with quartered cherry tomatoes and serve cut into slices with a mixed salad, mustard and crusty bread.

PREPARATION AND COOKING TIME: 2 HOURS 20 MINUTES PLUS CHILLING

Spicy pork spare ribs with ginger and hoisin sauce

SERVES 4

If you can only buy long spare ribs, get your butcher to chop them in half.

1 large garlic clove, crushed
2.5 ml/¹/₂ tsp grated fresh root ginger
1.5 ml/¹/₄ tsp chilli powder
2 spring onions (scallions), very finely chopped
45 ml/3 tbsp hoisin sauce
30 ml/2 tbsp medium-dry sherry
15 ml/1 tbsp soy sauce
5 ml/1 tsp clear honey
12 short Chinese pork spare ribs, about 550 g/1¹/₄ lb
30 ml/2 tbsp sunflower oil
15 ml/1 tbsp cornflour (cornstarch)
15 ml/1 tbsp water

① Mix the garlic, ginger, chilli powder, half the onions, the hoisin sauce, sherry, soy sauce and honey in a shallow dish that will fit in or over a steamer. Add the ribs and turn to coat completely. Leave to marinate for at least 2 hours.

② Heat the oil in a large frying pan (skillet). Drain the ribs and brown quickly on all sides.

③ Return to the dish and coat in the marinade again. Cover with foil, then transfer to a steamer, cover with a lid and steam for 1¹/₂ hours until the meat is really tender, turning the ribs over in the sauce halfway through cooking.

④ Blend the cornflour with the water in a small saucepan. Pour in the cooking juices and stir well. Bring to the boil and cook for 1 minute, stirring.

⑤ Transfer the ribs to warm plates. Spoon the sauce over and sprinkle with the remaining spring onion.

PREPARATION AND COOKING TIME: 1¾ HOURS PLUS MARINATING

Pork loin with cider, buttermilk and vegetables
SERVES 6

Pop the potatoes in a tier over the meat halfway through cooking.

700 g/1½ lb piece of boneless pork loin, rind removed
300 ml/½ pt/1¼ cups buttermilk
150 ml/¼ pt/²/₃ cup medium-sweet cider
30 ml/2 tbsp soy sauce
1 bay leaf
15 ml/1 tbsp chopped fresh sage
Salt and freshly ground black pepper
30 ml/2 tbsp sunflower oil
3 celery sticks, sliced
2 large carrots, sliced
15 ml/1 tbsp cornflour (cornstarch)
30 ml/2 tbsp water
5 ml/1 tsp caster (superfine) sugar
To serve:
New potatoes

① Wipe the meat and place in a deep dish. Mix the buttermilk with the cider and soy sauce and pour over. Add the bay leaf and sage and a sprinkling of salt and pepper. Turn the meat to coat completely. Cover and leave in the fridge to marinate for 24 hours, turning occasionally.

② Remove the meat from the marinade and wipe dry with kitchen paper (paper towels).

③ Heat the oil in a deep frying pan (skillet) and brown the meat on all sides.

④ Place the celery and carrots on a large sheet of foil. Top the vegetables with the meat and spoon over half of the marinade. Draw the foil up over the meat and vegetables and seal securely.

⑤ Transfer to a steamer, cover with a lid and steam for 1¼ hours or until really tender. Carefully lift the parcel out of the steamer, taking care not to spill the juices. Pour these into the pan the meat was browned in. Transfer the meat and vegetables to a carving dish and keep warm.

⑥ Pour the remaining marinade into the pan. Blend the cornflour with the water and stir into the marinade with the sugar. Bring to the boil and cook for 1 minute, stirring. Discard the bay leaf. Taste the sauce and season to taste.

⑦ Carve the meat and serve with the vegetables, sauce and new potatoes.

PREPARATION AND COOKING TIME: 1½ HOURS PLUS MARINATING

Peppered steaks with onion marmalade
SERVES 4

450–550 g/1–1¼ lb piece of beef fillet, cut into 4 steaks
45 ml/3 tbsp mixed pink green and black peppercorns,
  coarsely crushed
15 ml/1 tbsp sunflower oil
Salt
15 g/½ oz/1 tbsp butter or margarine
2 large onions, halved and thinly sliced
45 ml/3 tbsp caster (superfine) sugar
Finely grated rind and juice of 1 orange
30 ml/2 tbsp balsamic vinegar
Sprigs of fresh parsley, for garnishing
To serve:
Baby New Potatoes with Mint and Garlic Butter
  (see page 95) and a crisp green salad

① Coat the steaks in the crushed peppercorns. Heat the oil in a frying pan (skillet) and fry the beef very quickly on both sides to brown.

② Transfer the steaks to squares of foil. Sprinkle very lightly with salt, if liked. Wrap and place in a steamer. Cover with a lid and steam for 10–30 minutes, depending on how well you like your steak cooked.

③ Melt the butter or margarine in the frying pan. Add the onions and fry (sauté), stirring, for 3 minutes. Add the sugar and continue to fry, stirring occasionally, for about 5 minutes until a rich golden brown and the onions are soft.

④ Stir in the orange rind and juice and the balsamic vinegar. Stir for 1 minute until rich and thick. Remove from the heat.

⑤ Transfer the steaks to warm plates and spoon the onion marmalade to one side. Garnish with parsley sprigs and serve with Baby New Potatoes with Mint and Garlic Butter, and a crisp green salad.

PREPARATION AND COOKING TIME: 20–40 MINUTES

Lamb medallions with redcurrant and mint jus and turnip mash

SERVES 4

500 g/1¼ lb potatoes, cut into small chunks
2 large turnips, cut into small chunks
Salt and freshly ground black pepper
30 ml/2 tbsp redcurrant jelly (clear conserve)
30 ml/2 tbsp bottled garden mint sauce
300 ml/½ pt/1¼ cups lamb or beef stock, made with
  1 stock cube
400 g/14 oz lamb neck fillet, cut into 24 slices
15 ml/1 tbsp cornflour (cornstarch)
15 ml/1 tbsp water
15 g/½ oz/1 tbsp butter or margarine
15 ml/1 tbsp milk
Sprigs of fresh parsley or fresh redcurrants, for garnishing
To serve:
Mangetout (snow peas)

① Put the vegetables in a pan of salted water and bring to the boil, or place in a steamer tier and sprinkle with salt.

② Put a bowl over the saucepan or if using an electric steamer, place the rice bowl on top. Add the redcurrant jelly and stir until melted. Add the mint and stock. Stir and add the lamb. Cover with a lid and steam for 10 minutes.

③ Blend the cornflour and water in a small saucepan. When the meat is cooked, stir the cooking liquid into the saucepan. Bring to the boil and cook, stirring, for 1 minute.

④ Drain the potatoes and turnips if necessary. Mash with the butter or margarine and milk. Re-season, then pile on warm plates.

⑤ Arrange the lamb to one side and spoon the sauce over. Garnish with parsley and serve with mangetout.

PREPARATION AND COOKING TIME: 30 MINUTES

Beef and shiitake mushroom dim sum with sherry dipping sauce
SERVES 4

These work well with minced (ground) pork, chicken or prawns (shrimp) instead of the beef. You can use ordinary button mushrooms, if you prefer.

225 g/8 oz/2 cups plain (all-purpose) flour
A pinch of salt
1 egg
100 g/4 oz lean minced beef
50 g/2 oz shiitake mushrooms, finely chopped
2 spring onions (scallions), finely chopped
1 garlic clove, crushed
1.5 ml/¼ tsp Chinese five-spice powder
60 ml/4 tbsp soy sauce
4 cabbage or lettuce leaves, rinsed but not dried
1 red chilli, seeded and finely chopped
60 ml/4 tbsp medium-dry sherry
20 ml/4 tsp soft light brown sugar
1 thin sliver of fresh root ginger
10 ml/2 tsp cornflour (cornstarch)

① Put the flour and salt in a bowl. Beat the egg with 90 ml/ 6 tbsp water and work into the flour to form a firm dough. Knead gently on a lightly floured surface.

② Roll the dough into a sausage shape and cut into 20 slices. Roll out each slice into a 7.5 cm/3 in round.

③ Cover with a damp cloth while preparing the filling.

④ Mix the meat, mushrooms, one of the spring onions, the garlic and five-spice powder, using your hands to work it well together. Moisten with 30 ml/2 tbsp of the soy sauce.

⑤ Divide the mixture between the pieces of dough. Dampen the edges and fold over, pressing them well together to seal, forming semi-circular parcels. Put each one on a small square of non-stick baking parchment.

⑥ Line a steamer container with the cabbage or lettuce leaves. Arrange the dim sum parcels on top. Transfer to a steamer, cover tightly with a lid and steam for 25 minutes until cooked through.

⑦ Meanwhile, put the remaining soy sauce in a small saucepan with the chilli, sherry, sugar and ginger. Blend the cornflour with 30 ml/2 tbsp water and stir in. Bring to the boil, stirring until thickened slightly, then reduce the heat and simmer for 1 minute. Discard the ginger and pour into four small dishes.

⑧ Put the dim sum into warm bowls with the lettuce or cabbage, if liked. Sprinkle with the remaining spring onion and serve with the dipping sauce.

PREPARATION AND COOKING TIME: 50 MINUTES

Leg of lamb with feta and olives
SERVES 4

15 ml/1 tbsp olive oil
1 kg/2¼ lb half-leg of lamb
1 large garlic clove, cut into slivers
2 beefsteak tomatoes, skinned and chopped
900 g/2 lb potatoes, cut into large chunks
5 ml/1 tsp dried oregano
Salt and freshly ground black pepper
50 g/2 oz/⅓ cup black olives
50 g/2 oz/⅓ cup Feta cheese, crumbled
30 ml/2 tbsp chopped fresh parsley or coriander
  (cilantro), to garnish
To serve:
A mixed salad

① Heat the oil in a frying pan (skillet) and brown the lamb all over. Make slits in the meat and push in the slivers of garlic.

② Line the base and sides of a steamer container with foil, forming a bowl. Put the tomatoes in the base. Put the lamb on top and arrange the potatoes around. Season with salt and pepper and sprinkle the lamb with the oregano.

③ Put on the lid and steam for 2½ hours. Sprinkle the olives over, then re-cover and steam for a further 30 minutes.

④ Transfer the potatoes and olives to warm plates and sprinkle with the Feta cheese. Keep the plates warm while you transfer the meat to a carving dish. Pour the tomatoes and liquid into a small saucepan and boil rapidly for several minutes to reduce slightly. Season to taste.

⑤ Cut the meat into pieces (it will fall off the bones). Arrange on the plates with the potatoes and olives. Spoon the tomato juices over the meat, sprinkle with parsley or coriander and serve with a mixed salad.

PREPARATION AND COOKING TIME: ABOUT 3½ HOURS

Moussaka slippers
SERVES 4

2 large aubergines (eggplants)
1 onion, finely chopped
1 garlic clove, crushed
175 g/6 oz minced (ground) lamb or beef
30 ml/2 tbsp tomato purée (paste)
1.5 ml/¼ tsp ground cinnamon
2.5 ml/½ tsp dried oregano
30 ml/2 tbsp water
A good pinch of caster (superfine) sugar
Salt and freshly ground black pepper
1 egg
90 ml/6 tbsp plain yoghurt
30 ml/2 tbsp grated Cheddar cheese
15 ml/1 tbsp sliced stoned (pitted) black or green olives
To serve:
A mixed salad and daktalya or other crusty bread

① Halve the aubergines lengthways. Place in a steamer, cover with a lid and steam for 10 minutes. Lift out and leave to cool, scoop out most of the aubergine, leaving a wall all round. Chop the scooped-out flesh.

② Put the onion, garlic and meat in a saucepan and cook, stirring all the time, until the lamb is no longer pink and all the grains are separate. Stir in the chopped aubergine, tomato purée, cinnamon, oregano, water and sugar and add salt and pepper to taste.

③ Put the aubergines in a shallow dish that will fit in or over a steamer. Pack the meat mixture into the aubergines.

④ Beat the egg with the yoghurt and a little salt and pepper. Spoon over the meat mixture. Sprinkle with the cheese and olives. Cover the dish with foil. Steam for 30 minutes.

⑤ Transfer to warm plates. Serve with salad and crusty bread.

PREPARATION AND COOKING TIME: 55 MINUTES

Paprika chicken with vegetables

SERVES 4

1.5 kg/3 lb oven-ready chicken
1 onion
2 cloves
15 ml/1 tbsp paprika
Salt and freshly ground black pepper
450 g/1 lb small waxy potatoes, scrubbed
16 button (pearl) onions, peeled but left whole
225 g/8 oz baby carrots, scraped
1 corn cob, cut into 4 pieces
15 ml/1 tbsp cornflour (cornstarch)
300 ml/½ pt/1¼ cups chicken stock, made with 1 stock cube
30 ml/2 tbsp chopped fresh parsley

① Wipe the chicken inside and out with kitchen paper (paper towels). Pull out any fat from inside the body cavity. Stud the onion with the cloves and push inside the bird. Rub the paprika all over the skin and sprinkle with salt.

② Place in an electric steamer with the juice collector underneath or in a shallow dish in a steamer container over a saucepan. Cover with a lid and steam for 45 minutes.

③ Arrange the prepared vegetables around the chicken or in a steamer tier placed on top. Sprinkle with salt.

④ Cover again and steam for a further 45 minutes or until the chicken and vegetables are tender.

⑤ Transfer the chicken to a carving dish and the vegetables to a serving dish and keep warm.

⑥ Pour the cooking juices into a small saucepan. Whisk in the cornflour. Gradually add the stock, bring to the boil and cook for 1 minute, stirring until thickened. Stir in the parsley and season to taste.

⑦ Carve the chicken and transfer to warm plates. Spoon the sauce over and serve with the vegetables.

PREPARATION AND COOKING TIME: 1 HOUR 40 MINUTES

Turkey and ham rolls with asparagus sauce

SERVES 4

15 g/¹/₂ oz/1 tbsp butter or margarine
4 turkey breast steaks, about 150 g/5 oz each
4 slices of lean cooked ham
10 ml/2 tsp Dijon mustard
15 ml/1 tbsp chopped fresh sage
Salt and freshly ground black pepper
300 g/11 oz/1 medium can of cut asparagus, drained,
   reserving the liquid
15 ml/1 tbsp chopped fresh parsley
150 ml/¹/₄ pt/²/₃ cup crème fraîche
A few whole fresh chive stalks
To serve:
New potatoes and French (green) beans

① Grease four 20 cm/8 in squares of foil with the butter or margarine.

② Put the steaks one at a time in a polythene bag and beat with a rolling pin or meat mallet to flatten. Lay a slice of ham on each and trim to fit, if necessary. Spread with the mustard and sprinkle with the sage.

③ Roll up one steak at a time and season lightly with salt and pepper. Wrap each tightly in a square of buttered foil, sealing the ends well. Transfer the parcels to a steamer, cover with a lid and steam for 20 minutes.

④ Meanwhile, purée the asparagus pieces with the parsley in a blender or food processor. Tip into a saucepan and stir in the crème fraîche. Heat through, stirring. Season to taste. Thin, if necessary with a little of the asparagus liquid.

⑤ Unwrap the turkey rolls and cut each into four slices. Spoon the asparagus sauce on to four warm plates and arrange the turkey rolls on top. Garnish with a few chive stalks and serve with new potatoes and French beans.

PREPARATION AND COOKING TIME: 40 MINUTES

Chicken parcels with rosemary, garlic and mediterranean vegetables

SERVES 4

It is best to cook the parcels in two steamer tiers, but if you only have one, place the chicken parcels on top of the vegetable parcels, making sure steam can circulate.

60 ml/4 tbsp olive oil
Finely grated rind and juice of ½ lemon
15 ml/1 tbsp clear honey
15 ml/1 tbsp chopped fresh rosemary
1 garlic clove, crushed
Salt and freshly ground black pepper
4 skinless chicken breasts
12 baby new potatoes, scrubbed and sliced thinly
2 red onions, quartered
1 red (bell) pepper, cut into quarters
1 yellow pepper, cut into quarters
2 large courgettes (zucchini), cut diagonally into slices
Salt and freshly ground black pepper
30 ml/2 tbsp water

① Put 30 ml/2 tbsp of the oil in a shallow dish (make sure that it is large enough to hold the chicken pieces in a single layer). Whisk in the lemon rind and juice, the honey, rosemary, garlic and a little salt and pepper.

② Make several diagonal slashes along each chicken breast, without cutting right through. Lay the breasts in the marinade, then turn to coat completely. Cover and leave to marinate for 1 hour.

③ Cut four large squares of foil or double-thickness greaseproof (waxed) paper. Brush with a little of the marinade. Lay the potatoes in a single layer over one half of each piece of foil or paper. Sprinkle lightly with salt. Top each with a chicken breast and spoon any remaining marinade over. Fold the foil or paper over the top and twist and fold all round to make secure parcels.

④ Brush another large square of foil or double-thickness greaseproof paper with a little of the remaining oil. Separate the layers of onion and arrange on one half of the foil or paper with the pepper pieces and courgettes. Drizzle the remaining oil over. Sprinkle with salt and pepper and add the water. Fold the foil or paper over and twist and fold to seal all round.

⑤ Put the vegetable parcels in a steamer, cover with a lid and steam for 15 minutes.

⑥ Add the chicken parcels, then cover again and steam for 25 minutes or until the chicken and vegetables are cooked.

⑦ Open up the chicken parcels and carefully slide the contents on to warm plates. Scatter pieces of the Mediterranean vegetables around and serve straight away.

PREPARATION AND COOKING TIME: 1 HOUR PLUS MARINATING

Thai-style turkey curry with spring greens

SERVES 4

5 spring (collard) greens, thick stalks removed
2 eggs, beaten
250 ml/8 fl oz/1 cup coconut milk
15 ml/1 tbsp chopped fresh mint
15 ml/1 tbsp chopped fresh basil
30 ml/2 tbsp red curry paste
15 ml/1 tbsp Thai fish sauce
1 stalk of lemon grass, finely chopped
2.5 ml/$\frac{1}{2}$ tsp grated fresh root ginger
1 red chilli, seeded and chopped
Salt and freshly ground black pepper
450 g/1 lb turkey stir-fry meat
A few torn coriander (cilantro) leaves, for garnishing
To serve:
Coconut and Cardamom Rice (see page 68)

① Blanch the greens in boiling water for 3 minutes. Drain, rinse with cold water and drain again. Use to line a 1.2 litre/ 2 pt/5 cup dish that will fit in or over a steamer.

② Beat the eggs and coconut milk with the herbs, curry paste, fish sauce, lemon grass, ginger, chilli and some salt and pepper.

③ Cut up any large pieces of turkey, then stir the meat into the egg mixture.

④ Spoon into the lined dish and cover tightly with foil.

⑤ Place in or over the steamer, cover with a lid and steam for 1 hour until set.

⑥ Scatter a few torn coriander leaves over to garnish and serve with Coconut and Cardamom Rice.

PREPARATION AND COOKING TIME: 1 HOUR 10 MINUTES

Duck breasts with blueberries and mild blue cheese fondue

SERVES 4

4 duck breasts, with skin
Salt and freshly ground black pepper
5 ml/1 tsp paprika
100 g/4 oz fresh blueberries
30 ml/2 tbsp port
100 g/4 oz creamy blue cheese, such as Dolcelatte,
    Castello or Bresse Bleu, rinded and diced
5 ml/1 tsp cornflour (cornstarch)
120 ml/4 fl oz/½ cup crème fraîche
45 ml/3 tbsp milk
2.5 ml/½ tsp grated onion
To serve:
New potatoes and a rocket salad

① Rub the duck skin with a little salt and pepper and the paprika. Heat a frying pan (skillet) and cook the duck for about 3 minutes until golden brown on all sides. Transfer to a large sheet of foil, skin-sides up.

② Add the blueberries and port and draw the foil up over the duck, sealing the edges firmly together. Place in a steamer, cover with a lid and steam for 30 minutes.

③ Place the cheese in a small bowl with the cornflour, crème fraîche, milk and onion. Add a good grinding of pepper. Place either in the same tier as the duck (after 30 minutes) or in a tier above it. Cover with a lid and steam for a further 30 minutes. Stir the cheese mixture after 15 minutes.

④ Remove the duck and the cheese fondue from the steamer and beat the cheese mixture well.

⑤ Place a piece of duck on each of four plates and spoon the juices over. Trickle the blue cheese fondue around and serve with new potatoes and a rocket salad.

PREPARATION AND COOKING TIME: 1¼ HOURS

Pheasant in red wine with mushrooms and lardons

SERVES 4

1 oven-ready cock pheasant, quartered and skinned
50 g/2 oz smoked lardons
1 onion, finely chopped
100 g/4 oz baby button mushrooms
200 ml/7 fl oz/scant 1 cup red wine
15 ml/1 tbsp brandy
5 ml/1 tsp caster (superfine) sugar
Salt and freshly ground black pepper
1 bouquet garni sachet
30 ml/2 tbsp cornflour (cornstarch)
30 ml/2 tbsp water
30 ml/2 tbsp chopped fresh parsley, for garnishing
To serve:
New potatoes and Brussels sprouts

① Heat a frying pan (skillet), add the lardons, onion and mushrooms and cook, stirring, until the fat runs and the bacon is turning lightly golden.

② Put the pheasant in a heatproof dish that will fit in or over a steamer. Spoon the lardon mixture over.

③ Pour in the wine and brandy and sprinkle with the sugar and a little salt and pepper. Tuck the bouquet garni in amongst the pieces of pheasant.

④ Cover with foil, twisting and folding it under the rim of the dish to secure, then transfer to a steamer, cover with a lid and steam for 45 minutes. Turn the pieces of pheasant over in the wine. Re-cover and steam for a further 30–40 minutes until moist and tender.

⑤ Blend the cornflour with the water in a small saucepan. Pour in the pheasant cooking juices. Bring to the boil, stirring all the time until thickened. Cook for 1 minute. Taste and re-season, if necessary.

⑥ Transfer the pheasant to warm plates. Spoon the thickened sauce over, sprinkle with chopped parsley and serve with new potatoes and Brussels sprouts.

PREPARATION AND COOKING TIME: ABOUT 1½ HOURS

Lemon chicken bites with pesto sauce
SERVES 4

15 ml/1 tbsp water
15 ml/1 tbsp cornflour (cornstarch)
45 ml/3 tbsp ready-made pesto sauce
30 ml/2 tbsp medium-dry white wine
Salt and freshly ground black pepper
8 chicken thighs, skinned and chopped in half
½ lemon, thinly sliced
Sprigs of fresh basil, for garnishing
To serve:
Wild rice mix and a tomato and onion salad

① Mix the water and cornflour together in a large bowl. Stir in the pesto, wine and a little salt and pepper.

② Add the chicken pieces to the pesto mixture and turn to coat completely. Cover and leave to marinate in the fridge for at least 30 minutes, or overnight, if possible.

③ Pack the chicken pieces in a single layer into a shallow dish that will fit in or over a steamer. Pour over any marinade. Tuck in half of the lemon slices and cover tightly with foil.

④ Place in the steamer, cover with a lid and steam for 20 minutes. Turn the chicken over in the marinade and cook for a further 25 minutes or until the chicken is cooked through and tender. Discard the cooked pieces of lemon.

⑤ Transfer the chicken and sauce to warm plates, garnish with sprigs of basil and the remaining lemon slices and serve with wild rice mix and a tomato and onion salad.

PREPARATION AND COOKING TIME: 55 MINUTES PLUS MARINATING

Rice, Grains and Pasta

*R*ice, grains and pasta can all be cooked to perfection in a steamer. This chapter tells you how to prepare and serve them either plain or as part of a mouth-watering array of dishes – mostly savoury but a few sweet sensations too.

Steaming, rather than boiling, means that you avoid the messy business of the starchy water bubbling all over your hob. You are also less likely to overcook things – a plus for those of you who are used to sticky-based saucepans and soggy clumps of gluey rice or flabby pasta!

Steaming rice and wild rice mix

Follow this step-by-step guide for perfect fluffy results.

It is easiest to measure the rice and liquid (water or stock) in a measuring jug to get the volumes correct but I've given you the dry measures too in case you prefer to weigh it out.

① Measure the volume of rice you require in the jug:

1 serving = 50 ml/ 2 fl oz/¼ cup rice (50 g/2 oz/¼ cup, dry weight)

2 servings = 120 ml/4 fl oz/½ cup rice (100 g/4 oz/½ cup, dry weight)

4 servings = 250 ml/8 fl oz /1 cup rice (225 g/8 oz/1 cup, dry weight)

6 servings = 375 ml/13 fl oz/1½ cups rice (350 g/12 oz/ 1½ cups, dry weight)

② Put the rice into a bowl, cover with plenty of cold water and leave to soak for at least 30 minutes to wash out the excess starch.

③ Stir, then drain thoroughly.

④ Measure the volume of boiling water or stock needed: use 1½ parts liquid to 1 part rice.

1 serving = 90 ml/6 tbsp
2 servings = 175 ml/6 fl oz/¾ cup
4 servings = 375 ml/13 fl oz /1½ cups
6 servings = 500 ml/17 fl oz /2¼ cups

⑤ Put the rinsed, drained rice and measured liquid in a saucepan or the rice bowl in an electric steamer. Add a little salt, if liked.

⑥ Cover tightly with foil before adding a tight-fitting lid. If using a saucepan, put over the lowest possible heat. Steam for 25 minutes, then remove from the heat. Leave to stand, covered, for 5 minutes, fluff up and serve.

Note: Brown rice will need a longer cooking time – 45 minutes – to become tender.

Sticky rice
SERVES 4

Sticky rice is ideal for easy eating with chopsticks because it stays together in clumps! It can also be used for desserts (see page 68).

225 g/8 oz/1 cup Thai fragrant rice or other round-grain rice
Salt (optional)

① Put the rice in a bowl, cover with cold water and soak for at least 2 hours, preferably longer. Drain, rinse and drain again.

② Put a clean cloth (I use a new disposable washing-up cloth) in a steamer. Spread the rice in an even layer on the cloth. Sprinkle very lightly with salt if serving as a savoury accompaniment.

③ Cover with a lid and steam for 45 minutes. The rice should be just tender but still with some 'bite'.

④ Turn into a serving dish, cover and leave to stand for about 15 minutes until warm and sticky before serving.

PREPARATION AND COOKING TIME: 50 MINUTES
PLUS SOAKING AND STANDING

Sweet sticky rice balls
SERVES 4–6

These are delicious served with any fresh, sliced fruits –
mangoes, pawpaws and kiwifruit are particularly good.

1 quantity of freshly cooked sticky rice (see page 67)
15 ml/1 tbsp clear honey
100 g/4 oz/1 cup toasted sesame seeds

1. Turn the freshly cooked rice into a serving dish and while still hot, stir in the honey. Cover and leave to stand for about 15 minutes until just warm.

2. Shape into 12 small balls and roll in the sesame seeds.

PREPARATION AND COOKING TIME: 55 MINUTES
PLUS SOAKING AND STANDING

Coconut and cardamom rice
SERVES 4

225 g/8 oz/1 cup long-grain rice
4 spring onions (scallions), finely chopped
50 g/2 oz creamed coconut, finely chopped
375 ml/11 fl oz/1½ cups hot chicken or vegetable stock,
  made with 1 stock cube
4 cardamom pods
10 ml/2 tsp sunflower oil

1. Put the rice in a saucepan or in the bowl of a rice cooker in an electric steamer. Add the remaining ingredients and stir well. Cover tightly with foil, then a lid. Steam for 25 minutes (if you are using a saucepan, make sure the heat is very low) or until the liquid has been absorbed. Leave to stand, still covered with foil, for 5 minutes.

2. Discard the cardamom pods, fluff up well with a fork to distribute the melted coconut and serve.

PREPARATION AND COOKING TIME: 30 MINUTES PLUS STANDING

Chorizo and chicken paella

SERVES 4

If you are making this in an electric steamer, you will need to start the dish in a frying pan (skillet) for steps 1 and 2, then tip it into the rice bowl in the steamer and continue as below.

15 ml/1 tbsp olive oil
1 onion, chopped
1 garlic clove, crushed
4 chicken thighs, skinned and chopped in half
225 g/8 oz/1 cup long-grain rice
2.5 ml/½ tsp ground turmeric
600 ml/1 pt/2½ cups hot chicken stock, made with
  2 stock cubes
100 g/4 oz baby button mushrooms
100 g/4 oz chorizo sausage, sliced
200 g/7 oz/1 small can of pimientos, diced
50 g/2 oz frozen peas
2.5 ml/½ tsp dried oregano
Freshly ground black pepper
1 lemon, cut into wedges
30 ml/2 tbsp chopped fresh parsley

① Heat the oil in a large, shallow, heavy-based pan. Add the onion, garlic and chicken and fry (sauté) for 3 minutes, stirring and turning the chicken. Stir in the rice and saffron.

② Add the stock and bring to the boil.

③ Add all the remaining ingredients except the lemon and parsley. Cover tightly, reduce the heat to as low as possible and steam for 40 minutes. Stir and check that the liquid has been absorbed. The rice should be soft and moist, like a risotto. If not, re-cover and cook for a further few minutes.

④ Spoon on to warm plates, garnish with wedges of lemon and chopped parsley and serve.

PREPARATION AND COOKING TIME: 55 MINUTES

Wild mushroom pilaf with spicy coconut sauce

SERVES 4

If you are making this in an electric steamer, start it in a frying pan (skillet) for step 2, then tip it into the rice bowl and continue. There's no need to bring it to the boil before steaming. Packs of mixed mushrooms are widely available in supermarkets.

225 g/8 oz/1 cup basmati rice
30 ml/2 tbsp sunflower oil
2 onions, finely chopped
1 garlic clove, finely chopped
1 piece of preserved stem ginger in syrup, finely chopped
2.5 ml/½ tsp garam masala
100 g/4 oz mixed mushrooms (oyster, chestnut,
    chanterelle, etc.), trimmed and cut into pieces if large
600 ml/1 pt/2½ cups hot chicken or vegetable stock,
    made with 1 stock cube
Salt and freshly ground black pepper
1 fresh green chilli, finely chopped
2.5 ml/½ tsp ground turmeric
5 ml/1 tsp ground cumin
175 g/6 oz creamed coconut
5 ml/1 tsp caster (superfine) sugar
30 ml/2 tbsp chopped fresh coriander (cilantro)
Sprigs of fresh coriander and wedges of lime and tomato,
    for garnishing

① Soak the rice in plenty of cold water for at least 30 minutes, then stir well and drain thoroughly.

② Heat 15 ml/1 tbsp of the oil in a large saucepan. Add half the chopped onion and all the garlic and fry (sauté), stirring, for 3 minutes until lightly golden.

③ Add the rice, ginger and garam masala and stir for 1 minute until the rice is glistening. Add the mushrooms, 375 ml/13 fl oz/1½ cups of the stock and a little salt and pepper, stir and bring to the boil.

④ Cover tightly with foil, then the lid, turn down the heat as low as possible and steam for 25 minutes. Remove from the heat and leave to stand, still covered, for 5 minutes – without peeking!

⑤ Meanwhile, make the sauce. Heat the remaining oil in a small saucepan. Add the remaining onion and fry for 2 minutes, stirring.

⑥ Stir the spices into the onion and fry for 1 minute. Add the remaining stock and the creamed coconut. Cook, stirring, until the coconut has melted. Season to taste with the sugar, salt and pepper and simmer for 5 minutes, stirring occasionally. Stir in the chopped coriander.

⑦ Fluff up the pilaf with a fork and pile on to warm plates. Spoon the sauce around the rice and garnish with sprigs of coriander and wedges of lime and tomato.

PREPARATION AND COOKING TIME: ABOUT 35 MINUTES PLUS SOAKING

All-in-one risotto milanese

SERVES 4

Risottos are made normally by adding a little stock at a time. This version bypasses all that effort, but still creates a creamy, glorious dish.

1 onion, finely chopped
30 ml/2 tbsp olive oil
350 g/12 oz/1½ cups risotto rice
1.5 ml/½ tsp saffron powder
1 litre/1¾ pts/3¾ cups hot vegetable or chicken stock, made with 2 stock cubes
Salt and freshly ground black pepper
25 g/1 oz/2 tbsp unsalted (sweet) butter
15 g/½ oz/2 tbsp freshly grated Parmesan cheese
15 ml/1 tbsp chopped fresh parsley, for garnishing

① Fry (sauté) the onion in the oil in a small frying pan (skillet) for 2 minutes to soften. Stir in the rice until glistening. Tip into the rice bowl of an electric steamer or a bowl that will fit in or over a steamer.

② Stir in the saffron, stock and a little salt and pepper.

③ Cover with foil, then a lid, and steam for 30 minutes until most (but not all) of the liquid has been absorbed and the rice is tender but still has some 'bite'.

④ Stir in the butter and the Parmesan to form a creamy risotto and serve garnished with chopped parsley.

PREPARATION AND COOKING TIME: 40 MINUTES

Steamed porridge
SERVES 1

Porridge is much creamier when steamed instead of cooked directly in a saucepan and you won't have any impossibly sticky pans to wash up afterwards! You can make up to six portions in one go.

40 g/1½ oz/⅓ cup porridge oats
120 ml/4 fl oz/½ cup milk
120 ml/4 fl oz/½ cup boiling water
A pinch of salt
To serve:
Cream or milk with honey, brown sugar or golden (light corn) syrup

① Mix the oats, milk, water and salt together in a bowl over a pan of simmering water or in the rice bowl of an electric steamer.

② Cover with a lid and steam for 15–20 minutes, stirring occasionally, until thick and creamy.

③ Serve with cream or milk and sweeten to taste with honey, brown sugar or golden syrup.

PREPARATION AND COOKING TIME: ABOUT 20 MINUTES

Steamed couscous

SERVES 4

225 g/8 oz/1⅓ cups couscous
600 ml/1 pt/2½ cups boiling water or stock, made with
   1 stock cube
Salt

Method 1

This is ideal if you are cooking couscous to serve with a main dish that can be cooked underneath – the couscous can sit happily on the top until the main course is cooked. This method is more time-consuming than Method 2, but the results are worth it.

① Mix the couscous with the water and a pinch of salt or the stock. Leave to stand for 5 minutes to absorb the liquid.

② Line a steamer container with kitchen paper (paper towels) or a clean cloth and stand over a pan of gently simmering water or place in an electric steamer. Add the couscous and spread out. Cover with foil or a lid. Steam for 20 minutes or until ready to serve.

③ Tip into a serving dish. Fluff up with a fork and serve.

Method 2

This quicker method is ideal if you are going to press the couscous into moulds to be turned out on to serving plates or mix it with meat or other ingredients before serving.

① Mix the couscous with the water and salt or stock in a bowl and stand it over a pan of gently simmering water. Alternatively, place it in the rice bowl of an electric steamer.

② Cover with foil and a lid and steam for 10–20 minutes.

③ Fluff up with a fork and use as required.

Tabbouleh in crisp lettuce

SERVES 4

You'll think this has a lot of herbs in it, but you really do need them to get the gorgeous green, fragrant salad.

100 g/4 oz/1 cup bulgar (cracked wheat)
250 ml/8 fl oz/1 cup boiling water
Salt and freshly ground black pepper
75 ml/5 tbsp olive oil
45 ml/3 tbsp lemon juice
2 garlic cloves, crushed
50 g/2 oz chopped fresh parsley
50 g/2 oz chopped fresh mint
25 g/1 oz chopped fresh coriander (cilantro)
4 ripe tomatoes, very thinly sliced
5 cm/2 in piece of cucumber, peeled and very thinly sliced
2 little gem lettuces, separated into leaves
Wedges of lemon, for garnishing

① Put the bulgar in a bowl, stir in the boiling water and add 4 ml/¾ tsp salt. Cover with foil, transfer to a steamer, cover with a lid and steam for 20 minutes.

② Remove from the steamer, add a good grinding of pepper and stir in 45 ml/3 tbsp of the oil and all the lemon juice. Leave to cool.

③ Stir in the garlic and herbs, then taste and adjust the seasoning, if necessary. Cover and chill until ready to serve.

④ Arrange a circle of overlapping tomato and cucumber slices to one side of each of four plates. Pile the tabbouleh in the centre of the circle, leaving the edges of the tomato and cucumber just visible. Drizzle the remaining olive oil over. Arrange the lettuce leaves beside the tabbouleh. Garnish the plates with wedges of lemon.

PREPARATION AND COOKING TIME: 30 MINUTES PLUS CHILLING

Torta di polenta
SERVES 4

30 ml/2 tbsp olive oil
1 bunch of spring onions (scallions), cut into short lengths
2 garlic cloves, crushed
1 red (bell) pepper, thinly sliced
100 g/4 oz button mushrooms, sliced
425 g/15 oz/1 large can of cannellini beans, drained
425 g/15 oz/1 large can of artichoke hearts, drained
  and sliced
5 ml/1 tsp dried oregano
Salt and freshly ground black pepper
75 g/3 oz/½ cup polenta
50 g/2 oz/½ cup self-raising (self-rising) flour
5 ml/1 tsp baking powder
1 large egg
60 ml/4 tbsp single (light) cream
120 ml/4 fl oz/½ cup milk
450 ml/¾ pt/2 cups passata (sieved tomatoes)
2.5 ml/½ tsp dried basil
2.5 ml/½ tsp caster (superfine) sugar
A little grated Parmesan cheese, for garnishing
To serve:
Crusty bread and a green salad

① Heat all but 5 ml/1 tsp of the oil in a frying pan (skillet) and fry (sauté) the spring onions and half the garlic for 2 minutes. Add the pepper and mushrooms and fry for a further minute, stirring.

② Use the remaining oil to grease a 1.2 litre/2 pt/5 cup rectangular or oval heatproof dish that will fit in a steamer. Tip the onion mixture into the dish and stir in the drained beans and artichokes. Sprinkle with the oregano and a little salt and pepper.

③ Mix the polenta, flour, baking powder and a little salt and pepper in a bowl. Make a well in the centre and break in the egg. Add the cream and beat thoroughly until smooth, then stir in the milk to give a thick, smooth batter. Pour over the vegetables.

④ Cover with greased foil, with a pleat in the middle to allow for rising. Twist and fold all round to secure, or tie with string. Transfer to a steamer, cover with a lid and steam for 1 hour until risen and set.

⑤ Meanwhile, warm the passata with the remaining garlic, the basil, sugar and a little salt and pepper in a saucepan.

⑥ When the torta is cooked, remove the foil, dust with the Parmesan cheese and serve straight away with the tomato sauce, crusty bread and a green salad.

PREPARATION AND COOKING TIME: 1 HOUR 20 MINUTES

Corn morsels with sweet chilli dipping sauce
SERVES 4–6

These can be prepared ready for steaming, then stored in the fridge for up to 24 hours until required.

225 g/8 oz/2 cups cornmeal
250 ml/8 fl oz/1 cup chicken stock, made with 1 stock cube
2.5 ml/½ tsp salt
120 ml/4 fl oz/½ cup sunflower or corn oil, plus extra for greasing
225 g/8 oz pork sausagemeat
50 g/2 oz stuffed olives, finely chopped
1 onion, finely chopped
60 ml/4 tbsp tomato ketchup (catsup)
A few drops of Tabasco sauce
Freshly ground black pepper
For the sauce:
1 small green chilli, finely chopped
1 small garlic clove, crushed
120 ml/4 fl oz/½ cup passata (sieved tomatoes)
5 ml/1 tsp balsamic vinegar
10 ml/2 tsp clear honey
15 ml/1 tbsp snipped fresh chives, for garnishing

① Cut 16 squares of foil, each about 15 cm/6 in across, and brush thoroughly with oil.

② Put the cornmeal in a bowl and beat in the stock, salt, and oil to form a paste.

③ Spoon the paste on to the squares of foil and spread out, leaving a good 2.5 cm/1 in border all round.

④ Mix together the sausagemeat, olives, onion, half the ketchup and the Tabasco and a good grinding of pepper (you may find it easier to use your hands).

⑤ Divide the mixture into 16 portions. Put a portion on one half of each paste square, not quite to the edges.

⑥ Fold the foil over so the edges of the paste meet, then seal the foil parcels all round.

⑦ Arrange in a steamer in layers, so steam can circulate. Use two tiers if necessary. Cover with a lid and steam for 45 minutes. If using two tiers, switch their positions halfway through cooking.

⑧ Meanwhile, make the chilli sauce. Mix the remaining tomato ketchup with the chilli, garlic, passata, balsamic vinegar and honey. Cover and leave to stand to allow the flavours to develop while the parcels cook.

⑨ Carefully unwrap the morsels, arrange on plates, sprinkle with snipped chives and serve with the chilli sauce.

PREPARATION AND COOKING TIME: 1 HOUR 5 MINUTES

Steamed pasta
SERVES 4

This method is really only suitable for pasta shapes. Electric steamer manufacturers say you can cook long varieties this way, but you have to break them up to fit them in the rice bowl, which defeats the object of having long strands! Long varieties are best cooked in boiling, salted water with the sauce steamed over the top in a steamer tier (see recipes on pages 81 and 84).

225 g/8 oz pasta shapes
15 ml/1 tbsp olive oil
600 ml/1 pt/2½ cups cold water
Salt

① Mix the pasta with the oil and place in a bowl that will fit in or over a steamer or in the rice bowl of an electric steamer.

② Add the cold water and stir well. Cover tightly and steam for 20 minutes. Stir, then steam for a further 20 minutes until the pasta is just cooked.

③ Drain, rinse with boiling water, drain again and serve.

PREPARATION AND COOKING TIME: 40–45 MINUTES

Chickpea couscous with sweet spiced lamb and raisin sauce

SERVES 4

If you are using an electric steamer, cook the meat sauce in a pan to step 2, then tip it into a heatproof dish that will fit in the steamer. Cover with foil, then place in the bottom tier with the couscous in the rice bowl on top.

1 onion, finely chopped
1 green (bell) pepper, finely chopped
1 garlic clove, finely chopped
225 g/8 oz minced (ground) lamb
50 g/2 oz/⅓ cup raisins
2.5 ml/½ tsp ground cinnamon
2.5 ml/½ tsp ground ginger
2.5 ml/½ tsp ground mace
750 ml/1¼ pts/3 cups lamb or chicken stock, made with
   1 stock cube
250 ml/8 fl oz/1 cup passata (sieved tomatoes)
Salt and freshly ground black pepper
225 g/8 oz/1⅓ cups couscous
425 g/15 oz/1 large can of chickpeas (garbanzos), drained
15 ml/1 tbsp clear honey
30 ml/2 tbsp chopped fresh coriander (cilantro)

① Put the onion, green pepper, garlic and mince in a large saucepan. Cook, stirring, until all the grains of meat are separate and no longer pink.

② Stir in the raisins, spices, 150 ml/¼ pt/⅔ cup of the stock, the passata and a little salt and pepper. Bring to the boil, then turn down the heat to low.

③ Put the couscous in a bowl that will fit over the saucepan. Stir in the remaining stock and the chickpeas.

④ Cover and steam for 20 minutes.

⑤ Lift off the bowl of couscous. Stir the lamb sauce and add the honey. Taste and add more salt and pepper, if necessary.

⑥ Spoon the meat sauce on to warm plates. Press the couscous into small oiled bowls, then turn out in mounds on the meat sauce (or neatly pile the couscous up in the centre of the sauce). Scatter the coriander over and serve.

PREPARATION AND COOKING TIME: 40 MINUTES

Spaghetti with salsa alfredo
SERVES 4

225 g/8 oz spaghetti
15 ml/1 tbsp olive oil
300 ml/½ pt/1¼ cups double (heavy) cream
50 g/2 oz/¼ cup unsalted (sweet) butter, cut into small pieces
100 g/4 oz/1 cup freshly grated Parmesan cheese
Freshly ground black pepper
To serve:
A crisp green salad

① Bring a large pan of lightly salted water to the boil. Add the spaghetti and gradually push it gently so that it coils round in the pan as it softens. When all the pasta is submerged, stir gently and add the oil.

② Put the cream in a bowl with the butter and half the cheese and place in a steamer container on top of the pan. Cover and steam for 10 minutes.

③ Drain the pasta and return to the pan. Stir the sauce well and pour over the pasta. Toss well with a good grinding of pepper. Pile on warm plates and serve with the remaining cheese sprinkled over and a crisp green salad.

PREPARATION AND COOKING TIME: 15 MINUTES

Chinese noodle rolls

SERVES 4–6

You can wrap the unfilled noodle rolls loosely in foil and keep at room temperature all day, if necessary, before serving.

100 g/4 oz/1 cup plain (all-purpose) flour
15 ml/1 tbsp cornflour (cornstarch)
A good pinch of salt
A good pinch of Chinese five-spice powder
45 ml/3 tbsp sunflower oil, plus extra for greasing
300 ml/½ pt/1¼ cups cold water
For the filling:
1 bunch of spring onions (scallions), finely chopped
100 g/4 oz/2 cups beansprouts
1 red (bell) pepper, halved and cut into thin strips
1 carrot, coarsely grated
100 g/4 oz button mushrooms, thinly sliced
5 cm/2 in piece of cucumber, cut into thin matchsticks
A good pinch of ground ginger
15 ml/1 tbsp soy sauce
15 ml/1 tbsp medium-dry sherry
2.5 ml/½ tsp soft light brown sugar
30 ml/2 tbsp toasted sesame seeds and extra soy sauce,
   for garnishing

① Put the flour, cornflour, salt, spice and 30 ml/2 tbsp of the oil in a bowl. Beat in the water to form a smooth batter.

② Oil two 18 cm/7 in round sandwich tins (pans). Pour enough batter in each to coat the base and tilt so that it spreads out.

③ Transfer to a steamer in two tiers, cover and steam for 5 minutes. Remove the pans and stand the bases in cold water to cool the noodle cakes quickly. Loosen one edge, then roll up gently. Place on a plate and cover with foil.

④ Repeat oiling and steaming three more times, making eight noodle cakes in all.

⑤ Heat the remaining oil in a wok or saucepan. Reserve a little of the green chopped spring onion for garnishing, then add all the prepared vegetables for the filling to the oil and stir-fry for 3 minutes. Add the ginger, soy sauce, sherry and sugar and cook, stirring, for 2 minutes.

⑥ Unroll the noodle cakes, add the filling and roll up again. Cut each into three pieces and arrange on plates. Sprinkle with a little soy sauce, the reserved spring onion and the sesame seeds and serve.

PREPARATION AND COOKING TIME: 40 MINUTES

Quick macaroni cheese
SERVES 4

225 g/8 oz macaroni
600 ml/1 pt/2½ cups water
Salt and freshly ground black pepper
200 g/7 oz/scant 1 cup cheese spread
60 ml/4 tbsp milk
2 tomatoes, sliced

① Put the pasta in a flameproof dish that will fit in or over a steamer. Alternatively, use the rice bowl of an electric steamer. Add the water and a good pinch of salt and stir well.

② Cover loosely with foil and steam for 15 minutes. Stir well, re-cover and steam for a further 15 minutes until tender. Stir, then drain and return to the dish or turn into a serving dish if you used the rice bowl.

③ Stir in the cheese spread until melted, then thin with the milk.

④ Arrange the sliced tomatoes over the top. Either cover the dish with foil again and return to the steamer for 2–3 minutes to heat through or flash under a preheated grill (broiler) to heat through and lightly cook the tomatoes.

PREPARATION AND COOKING TIME: 40 MINUTES

Spaghetti alla rustica
SERVES 4

You can use a potato peeler to shave thin strips off a block of Parmesan.

225 g/8 oz spaghetti
Salt and freshly ground black pepper
90 ml/6 tbsp olive oil
2 garlic cloves, crushed
50 g/2 oz/1 small can of anchovies, chopped, reserving
  the oil
5 ml/1 tsp dried oregano
30 ml/2 tbsp roughly chopped fresh parsley
30 ml/2 tbsp roughly chopped fresh basil
50 g/2 oz/½ cup Parmesan shavings
To serve:
Crusty bread and a green salad

① Bring a large pan of water to the boil and add a pinch of salt. Add the spaghetti and gradually push it gently so that it coils round in the pan as it softens. When all the pasta is submerged, stir gently and add 15 ml/1 tbsp of the oil.

② Put the remaining oil, the garlic, anchovies and their oil and the oregano in a bowl and place in a steamer container on top of the pan. Cover and steam for 10 minutes, while the spaghetti cooks, stirring occasionally until the anchovies 'melt' into the oil.

③ Remove the steamer, then drain the spaghetti and return to the pan. Add the sauce and the fresh herbs and toss well.

④ Pile on to warm plates and garnish with the Parmesan shavings. Serve with crusty bread and a green salad.

PREPARATION AND COOKING TIME: 20 MINUTES

Marbled semolina pudding
SERVES 4

600 ml/1 pt/2½ cups milk
50 g/2 oz/½ cup semolina (cream of wheat)
25 g/1 oz/2 tbsp caster (superfine) sugar
60 ml/4 tbsp raspberry jam (conserve)

① Pour about a quarter of the milk into a saucepan. Blend in the semolina and sugar. Stir in the remaining milk and bring to the boil, stirring. Pour into a 900 ml/1½ pt/3¾ cup heatproof serving dish that will fit in or over a steamer.

② Spoon the jam over and mix just enough to give a marbled effect. Cover tightly with foil, twisting and folding it under the rim to secure. Transfer to the steamer, cover with a lid and steam for 30 minutes. Serve hot.

PREPARATION AND COOKING TIME: 35 MINUTES

Extra-creamy rice pudding
SERVES 4

50 g/2 oz/¼ cup pudding (round-grain) rice
25 g/1 oz/2 tbsp caster (superfine) sugar
410 g/14½ oz/1 large can of unsweetened condensed
  (evaporated) milk
A little grated nutmeg

① Put the rice in a 900 ml/1½ pt/3¾ cup heatproof dish that will fit in or over a steamer. Stir in the sugar, milk and half a can of water. Sprinkle with grated nutmeg. Cover the dish tightly with foil.

② Transfer the dish to a steamer, cover with a lid and steam for 3 hours, stirring halfway through cooking. Stir again before serving.

PREPARATION AND COOKING TIME: 3 HOURS 5 MINUTES

Chocolate chip rice moulds
SERVES 4

This is for serious chocoholics! You can also serve the rice moulds with my raspberry coulis (see page 31) instead of the chocolate sauce for a colourful, fruitier dessert.

100 g/4 oz/½ cup pudding (round-grain) rice
200 ml/7 fl oz/scant 1 cup milk
30 ml/2 tbsp double (heavy) cream
40 g/1½ oz//3 tbsp caster (superfine) sugar
5 ml/1 tsp vanilla essence (extract)
50 g/2 oz/½ cup chocolate chips
To serve:
Hot Chocolate Sauce (see page 152)

① Mix all the ingredients together and spoon into four lightly greased ramekin dishes (custard cups) or dariole moulds.

② Cover each securely with foil and place in a steamer. Cover with a lid and steam for 1 hour or until the rice is soft and has absorbed all the liquid. Meanwhile, make the sauce.

③ Leave the rice moulds to cool for 3 minutes, then loosen the edges and turn out on to warm plates. Spoon the chocolate sauce around and serve.

PREPARATION AND COOKING TIME: 1 HOUR 10 MINUTES

Vegetables

This chapter is full of tips on how to steam plain vegetables perfectly. There are also lots of gorgeous recipes for vegetable dishes, which may be used to serve as starters, as accompaniments to plain steamed, grilled (broiled), roasted or fried (sautéed) meats, poultry and fish – and, of course, to enhance the main courses in this book.

Preparation of vegetables for steaming

Wash and peel or scrub them, then cut large vegetables into even-sized pieces. Arrange in a steamer with the densest parts towards the centre. Don't over-fill the container – the steam must be allowed to circulate. The maximum quantity is enough for 4–6 people.

Method 1

Place them in an even layer in a steamer. Sprinkle with salt, if liked. Cover with a tightly fitting lid and steam until just tender. Stir or rearrange the vegetables once during cooking. Steaming will take about 5 minutes longer than boiling. Remember you can place vegetables in a steamer tier over the main-course meat, fish, poultry, etc.

Note: If using a pan with tiered steamers, boil dense vegetables that require longer cooking in the cooking water whilst steaming more tender ones in a container on top. If you are using an electric steamer, start steaming the longer-cooking foods first, then add the quicker cooking foods in the top tiers.

Method 2

Melt a knob of butter or margarine in a shallow pan. Add the vegetables in a single layer. Cover with a tight-fitting lid and shake the pan. Cook over a moderate heat for a few minutes until steam forms, then turn down the heat to low and cook until they are just tender, shaking the pan occasionally. Keep the heat low or the vegetables will burn on the base.

Steaming and serving vegetables

Vegetable	Preparation	Approximate Steaming time	Serving Suggestions
Artichokes, globe	Hold firmly and twist off the stalks. Trim the points of the leaves, if liked. Rub cut surfaces with lemon juice if not cooking immediately. To remove the choke, spread the top leaves apart and pull off the small inner leaves. Scrape out the hairy choke with a teaspoon, exposing the 'heart' below. The artichokes can now be stuffed, if liked.	*Method 1* With choke: 40–50 minutes Without choke, plain: 20–30 minutes Without choke, stuffed: 40–50 minutes	Serve hot with Hollandaise sauce or melted butter. Serve cold with vinaigrette dressing, mayonnaise or tartare sauce.
Artichokes, Jerusalem	Scrub or thinly peel. Cut into bite-sized pieces and toss in a little lemon juice.	*Method 1 or 2* 20–30 minutes	Serve plain, with white, parsley or cheese sauce or puréed with black pepper and a little cream or butter.
Asparagus	Trim the base of the stalks and scrape the stalks, if thick. Tie in neat bundles.	*Method 1* 10–25 minutes, depending on size	Serve hot with olive oil and shaved fresh Parmesan, melted butter, Hollandaise sauce or savoury mousseline sauce. Serve cold with vinaigrette dressing or garlic mayonnaise.
Beans, broad (fava)	Shell, if fresh, or cook from frozen.	*Method 1* 10–15 minutes	Serve plain or with parsley sauce.
Beans, flat	Top and tail. Cut into diagonal pieces, about 2.5 cm/1 in long, or slice diagonally, like runner beans.	*Method 1* 10–15 minutes	Serve plain or tossed in a little olive oil and finely chopped walnuts.

Vegetable	Preparation	Approximate Steaming time	Serving Suggestions
Beans, French (green)	Top and tail. Cut into short lengths, if liked.	*Method 1* 10–15 minutes	Serve hot, plain or tossed with a dash of soy sauce. Serve cold, sprinkled with finely chopped onion or shallot, olive oil and wine vinegar.
Beans, runner	String, then cut into diagonal thin slices.	*Method 1* 15 minutes	Serve plain or with a fresh tomato sauce.
Beetroot (red beets)	Choose only baby beets for steaming. Wash but do not peel. Cut off the leaves leaving short stalks. Do not cut off the roots.	*Method 1* 45 minutes–1 hour	Peel and cut off roots. Serve hot with white or parsley sauce. Serve cold in spiced vinegar or mayonnaise.
Broccoli	Cut into small, even-sized florets.	*Method 1* 15–20 minutes	Serve plain or in white, cheese or fresh tomato sauce.
Brussels sprouts	Trim off stalks and any damaged or tough outer leaves. Make a cross-cut into the base of each.	*Method 1* 10–15 minutes	Serve plain, tossed in butter with sautéed chestnuts or sprinkled with finely chopped crispy bacon.
Cabbage	Discard any damaged outer leaves. Finely shred, or cut into wedges, discarding any thick central stalk.	*Method 1* Wedges: 20 minutes Shredded: 10 minutes *Method 2* Shredded: 6–8 minutes	Method 1: Serve plain or tossed in butter or sprinkled with soy sauce. Method 2: Sprinkle with caraway seeds.
Carrots	Scrub, scrape or peel, depending on size. Leave baby ones whole. Cut larger ones into dice, slices or matchsticks.	*Method 1* 15–30 minutes, depending on size and age *Method 2* 10–15 minutes	Method 1: Serve plain or tossed in butter. Method 2: Toss in a little clear honey to glaze just before serving.
Cauliflower	Cut into small, even-sized florets. Small green leaves may be eaten, if liked, but discard thick stalks.	*Method 1* 15–20 minutes	Serve plain, with white or cheese sauce.

Vegetable	Preparation	Approximate Steaming time	Serving Suggestions
Celeriac (celery root)	Halve, peel, dice or cut into matchsticks. If it is to be served cold, coarsely grate or shred.	*Method 1* Pieces: 20–30 minutes Grated/shredded: 5 minutes	Serve pieces hot with white or Hollandaise sauce. Grated and shredded may be served cold, tossed in mayonnaise or French dressing.
Celery	Trim roots and leaves. Discard damaged outer stalks. Scrub and cut into short lengths. Cut hearts into quarters.	*Method 1 or 2* 20–25 minutes	Serve plain or in white, parsley or cheese sauce.
Chicory (Belgian endive)	Cut a cone-shaped core out of the base of each head. Leave whole or slice.	*Method 2* Sliced: 10 minutes Whole: 20–30 minutes	Serve plain or with a cheese sauce.
Corn cobs	Trim roots and discard husks and silks.	*Method 1* 20 minutes	Serve with melted butter or Hollandaise sauce.
Courgettes (zucchini)	Slice, dice or cut into matchsticks or halve, remove seeds and stuff.	*Method 1* Plain: 10–15 minutes Stuffed: 30 minutes *Method 2* 8–10 minutes, with a crushed garlic clove added, if liked	Method 1: Serve plain, with white, parsley, cheese or tomato sauce. Method 2: Serve sprinkled with chopped fresh herbs or grated cheese.
Cucumber	Cut into dice or matchsticks or halve, remove seeds, then stuff.	*Method 1* Plain: 10–15 minutes, Stuffed: 30 minutes	Serve with white, cheese, tarragon, dill, parsley, tomato, prawn or anchovy sauce.
Fennel	Trim off the feathery fronds and use for garnish. Trim bases, then slice or quarter lengthways.	*Method 1 or 2* Slices: 20 minutes Quarters: 30 minutes	Serve plain, or with white, cheese, herb or tomato sauce.
Kale	Shred, discarding any thick stalks.	*Method 1* 15 minutes	Serve plain or sprinkled with croûtons.
Kohl rabi	Peel and cut into even-sized chunks.	*Method 1 or 2* 40 minutes	Serve plain or with white sauce.
Leeks	Trim roots and green tops. Discard outer leaves. Split, wash thoroughly, then slice. Leave baby leeks whole.	*Method 1* 20–30 minutes, depending on size. *Method 2* (for baby leeks) 25 minutes	Serve plain or with white or cheese sauce. May also be served cold with vinaigrette dressing.

Vegetable	Preparation	Approximate Steaming time	Serving Suggestions
Mangetout (snow peas)	Top and tail, but leave whole.	*Method 1* 3–5 minutes	Serve plain or tossed in butter.
Marrow (squash)	Peel if old. Cut into rings (if stuffing), strips or dice, discarding seeds.	*Method 1 or 2* Plain: 20–40 minutes, depending on size and age *Method 1* Stuffed: 45–60 minutes	Serve plain or with white, cheese or tomato sauce.
Mushrooms	Wipe, peel if large. Trim stalks. Leave whole, quarter or slice, as appropriate.	*Method 1 or 2* 5–20 minutes, depending on size	Serve plain or with garlic butter or a cream or tomato sauce.
Okra (ladies' fingers)	Wash, but do not cut.	*Method 1 or 2* 20–30 minutes	Serve with butter or olive oil and lemon juice, flavoured with garlic, if liked or Hollandaise sauce.
Onions	Peel and leave baby ones whole, slice or chop large ones or scoop out and stuff.	*Method 1* Baby, whole or stuffed: 30–60 minutes *Method 2* Sliced or chopped: 5–10 minutes	Whole baby onions: serve plain or with white or cheese sauce. Stuffed: serve with white, cheese or tomato sauce. Chopped or sliced: serve plain.
Pak choi	Trim, but leave whole or halve lengthways, if large.	*Method 1* 15 minutes	Serve plain or sprinkled with a few drops of sesame oil and soy sauce.
Parsnips	Peel and cut into wedges or dice. Use only small, tender parsnips.	*Method 1* 30 minutes	Serve plain, mashed with butter and black pepper or in a cream sauce.
Peas, garden and sugar snap	Shell garden peas. Top and tail sugar snap peas but leave the pods.	*Method 1* 15–25 minutes, depending on age	Serve plain or tossed in butter.
(Bell) peppers	To serve plain, halve, remove seeds and slice or dice. To serve stuffed, cut off the tops, remove the seeds and stuff.	*Method 1* Sliced or diced: 10–15 minutes Stuffed: 45–60 minutes	Serve plain, with butter and/or sprinkled with chopped parsley or other herbs.
Potatoes	Peel and cut into chunks. New, small potatoes may be scrubbed or scraped and left whole. Cover with cold water until ready to cook.	*Method 1* 15–30 minutes, depending on size	Serve plain, with butter and/or sprinkled with chopped parsley or other herbs or mash with butter and milk.

Vegetable	Preparation	Approximate Steaming time	Serving Suggestions
Pumpkin	Peel and dice.	*Method 1* 30–40 minutes, depending on age	Serve with cheese sauce or mash with butter and black pepper. Also purée and sweeten for desserts.
Salsify and scorzonera (black salsify)	Peel and dice. Place in water with a little lemon juice added until ready to cook.	*Method 1* 30–40 minutes	Serve tossed in butter or with a white, cheese or Béarnaise sauce.
Swiss chard	Cut the green leaves off the stalks. Tie the stalks in a bundle, shred the leaves.	*Method 1* Stalks: 30 minutes Greens: 15–20 minutes	Serve stalks with melted butter or Hollandaise sauce (like asparagus); serve greens plain or with a white sauce.
Spinach	Wash thoroughly, discard thick stalks.	*Method 1* 5–10 minutes	Drain thoroughly. Chop after cooking, if liked. Serve plain or with a cream sauce.
Swede (rutabaga)	Peel thickly and dice.	*Method 1* 15–30 minutes, depending on size and age	Serve plain, tossed or mashed with butter and black pepper or ginger.
Sweet potatoes	Peel and dice or slice.	*Method 1* 20–40 minutes, depending on size	Serve plain or mash with butter and black pepper.
Tomatoes	Leave whole.	*Method 1* 10–15 minutes, depending on size, in a dish or on foil, to catch the juice *Method 2* 5–10 minutes, depending on size	Serve plain or with chopped fresh herbs.
Turnips	Peel thickly. Leave whole if 'baby' sized, dice if large.	*Method 1* 20–40 minutes, depending on size and age *Method 2* 15–20 minutes	Serve plain, tossed in butter or with white sauce.
Yams	Peel and dice. Cover with water with a little lemon juice added until ready to cook.	*Method 1* 20–40 minutes	Serve plain, with white sauce, or mashed with butter and black pepper.

Lebanese-style dolmas

SERVES 4

You can use vacuum-packed, canned or fresh vine leaves for this dish. If you use fresh, choose large leaves and blanch them in boiling water for 3 minutes first.

30 ml/2 tbsp chopped fresh parsley
15 ml/1 tbsp chopped fresh mint
4 spring onions (scallions), finely chopped
1 beefsteak tomato, finely chopped
50 g/2 oz/¼ cup pudding (round-grain) rice
Salt and freshly ground black pepper
A pinch of ground cinnamon
15 ml/1 tbsp lemon juice
15 ml/1 tbsp olive oil
12 vine leaves
250 ml/8 fl oz/1 cup vegetable stock, made with 1 stock cube
Wedges of lemon, for garnishing

① Mix together all the ingredients except for the vine leaves and stock.

② Divide the mixture among the vine leaves, spooning it towards the stalk end. Fold in the sides, then roll up tightly.

③ Pack the dolmas in a single layer in a dish that will fit in or over a steamer. Pour the stock over. Cover tightly with foil. Twist and fold under the rim to secure.

④ Transfer to the steamer, cover with a lid and steam for 45 minutes until cooked through. Leave to cool in the liquid, then drain. Chill, if liked, then serve garnished with wedges of lemon.

PREPARATION AND COOKING TIME: 55 MINUTES

Baby leeks with pine nuts

SERVES 4

These make a delicious accompaniment to plain cooked lamb chops, fish or chicken.

12 whole baby leeks, trimmed and thoroughly washed
Salt and freshly ground black pepper
50 g/2 oz/¼ cup butter or margarine
30 ml/2 tbsp toasted pine nuts
30 ml/2 tbsp chopped fresh parsley, for garnishing

① Lay the leeks in a steamer container. Sprinkle with salt and pepper. Transfer to a steamer, cover with a lid and steam for 20 minutes.

② Put the butter and pine nuts in a small bowl in the steamer or in the rice bowl of an electric steamer. Cover and steam with the leeks for a further 5 minutes until melted.

③ Put the leeks on plates and spoon the butter and nuts over. Garnish with parsley and serve.

PREPARATION AND COOKING TIME: 30 MINUTES

Steamed cherry tomatoes with basil

SERVES 4

225 g/8 oz cherry tomatoes
5 ml/1 tsp caster (superfine) sugar
Salt and freshly ground black pepper
15 ml/1 tbsp chopped fresh basil
15 ml/1 tbsp balsamic vinegar
5 ml/1 tsp tomato purée (paste)

① Put the tomatoes in a shallow dish that will fit in or over a steamer. Sprinkle with the sugar, a little salt and pepper, half the basil and the vinegar. Cover with foil.

② Transfer to a steamer, cover with a lid and steam for 5 minutes until cooked but still holding their shape.

③ Carefully transfer the tomatoes to a serving dish. Stir the tomato purée into the juices to thicken, then spoon over the tomatoes. Sprinkle with the remaining basil and serve.

PREPARATION AND COOKING TIME: 10 MINUTES

Baby new potatoes with mint and garlic butter
SERVES 4

450 g/1 lb baby new potatoes, scrubbed or scraped
2 large sprigs of fresh mint
Salt
1 large garlic clove, crushed
50 g/2 oz/¼ cup unsalted (sweet) butter
Freshly ground black pepper

① Place the potatoes in a steamer container with one of the sprigs of mint and a good sprinkling of salt. Transfer to a steamer, cover with a lid and steam for 15 minutes.

② Pull the leaves off the remaining sprig of mint and chop. Put in a small bowl with the garlic, butter and a good grinding of pepper. Put in the steamer with the potatoes. Re-cover and steam for a further 5 minutes or until the potatoes are tender and the butter has melted.

③ Tip the potatoes into a serving dish. Stir the butter mixture and pour over. Toss gently and serve.

PREPARATION AND COOKING TIME: 25 MINUTES

Potato, broad bean and parsley mash
SERVES 4

*You can use either frozen or fresh, shelled beans. If you want
a smoother mash, you can remove their skins.*

900 g/2 lb potatoes, cut into walnut-sized pieces
225 g/8 oz baby broad (fava) beans
Salt and freshly ground black pepper
15 g/½ oz/1 tbsp butter or margarine
60 ml/4 tbsp milk
30 ml/2 tbsp chopped fresh parsley

① Spread the potatoes and beans out in a steamer container.
Sprinkle with salt. Transfer to a steamer, cover with a lid
and steam for 25 minutes or until really tender.

② Tip the cooked vegetables into a bowl. Add the butter or
margarine and milk and mash thoroughly. Season to taste
and beat in the parsley.

PREPARATION AND COOKING TIME: 35 MINUTES

French-style peas with lettuce
SERVES 4

15 g/½ oz/1 tbsp butter or margarine
1 onion, very finely chopped
225 g/8 oz frozen peas
½ round or ¼ small iceberg lettuce, finely shredded
5 ml/1 tsp dried mint
Salt and freshly ground black pepper

① Melt the butter or margarine in the rice bowl of an electric
steamer or in a bowl that will fit in or over a steamer. Add
the remaining ingredients. Stir well.

② Cover the bowl with foil, transfer to the steamer, cover with
a lid and steam for 15–20 minutes, stirring once. Serve hot.

PREPARATION AND COOKING TIME: 20–25 MINUTES

Scalloped potatoes

SERVES 4

These potatoes will sit quite happily in the steamer for longer than their cooking time, so don't worry if other foods take slightly longer to cook.

---

15 g/¹/₂ oz/1 tbsp butter or margarine
450 g/1 lb potatoes, cut into thin slices
1 onion, thinly sliced
Salt and freshly ground black pepper
60 ml/4 tbsp milk
15 ml/1 tbsp chopped fresh parsley, for garnishing

---

① Grease a large sheet of foil with the butter or margarine.

② Layer the potato slices with the onion and salt and pepper in a square on the centre of the foil.

③ Spoon over the milk, then fold the foil up over the potatoes, sealing the edges well together. Transfer to a steamer.

④ Cover with a lid and steam for 30–40 minutes until cooked through (the time will depend on how thickly you layer the potatoes). Transfer to warm plates.

⑤ Spoon any cooking juices over and sprinkle with chopped parsley before serving.

PREPARATION AND COOKING TIME: 40–50 MINUTES

Spiced potato cakes
SERVES 4

These are ideal to serve with a grilled (broiled) or steamed meat or fish but are also lovely with a curry as a change from rice. Alternatively, top each with a steam-poached egg (see page 20) as a snack meal.

---

500 g/1 lb 2 oz potatoes, scrubbed
1 onion
5 ml/1 tsp ground cumin
2.5 ml/$^1\!/_2$ tsp ground coriander (cilantro)
2.5 ml/$^1\!/_2$ tsp salt
Freshly ground black pepper
30 ml/2 tbsp chopped fresh coriander
15 ml/1 tbsp chopped fresh parsley
1 egg, beaten
A little sunflower oil, for greasing

---

① Coarsely grate the potatoes into a colander. Squeeze thoroughly to remove excess liquid, then tip into a bowl.

② Grate the onion into the bowl and stir in the ground cumin and coriander, the salt, a good grinding of pepper and the herbs. Mix with the beaten egg.

③ Lightly oil four squares of foil. Shape the mixture into four flat cakes and place one on each piece of foil. Fold the foil over and seal the edges all round. Place in a steamer, cover with a lid and steam for 30 minutes until tender.

④ Slide on to warm plates and serve.

PREPARATION AND COOKING TIME: 40 MINUTES

Creamy cauliflower cheese
SERVES 4

This version avoids the hassle of making cheese sauce in a separate pan. To turn it into a lunch dish, warm a large, opened can of chopped tomatoes in the steamer at the same time as cooking the cauliflower and spoon it over before adding the cheese sauce. To lower the fat content, use reduced-fat cheese and skimmed milk. Try it with broccoli instead of cauliflower too.

1 small cauliflower, cut into small florets
Salt and freshly ground black pepper
100 g/4 oz/1 cup Cheddar cheese, grated
150 ml/¹/₄ pt/²/₃ cup milk
2.5 ml/¹/₂ tsp made English mustard
15 ml/1 tbsp cornflour (cornstarch)
30 ml/2 tbsp crushed cornflakes, for garnishing

① Put the cauliflower in a steamer and sprinkle with salt.

② Mix the cheese, milk, mustard and cornflour together in a small bowl. Add a little salt and pepper. Place in the steamer with the cauliflower (or in a separate tier, if necessary).

③ Cover with a lid and steam for 20 minutes or until the florets are just tender. Stir the sauce and rearrange the florets halfway through cooking.

④ Transfer the cauliflower to a warm serving dish. Stir the sauce well and spoon over the cauliflower. Sprinkle with crushed cornflakes and serve.

PREPARATION AND COOKING TIME: 25 MINUTES

Puy lentil and vegetable pot

SERVES 4

This is also delicious served cold, dressed with a little balsamic vinegar.

175 g/6 oz/1 cup Puy lentils
2 carrots OR ¼ small swede (rutabaga) OR 1 salsify, cut into small dice
1 red (bell) pepper, cut into small dice
2 courgettes (zucchini), cut into small dice
4 spring onions (scallions), chopped
300 ml/½ pt/1¼ cups hot vegetable stock, made with 1 stock cube
1 bay leaf
Salt and freshly ground black pepper
30 ml/2 tbsp chopped fresh parsley, for garnishing

① Rinse the lentils and place in a large bowl that will fit in or over a steamer. Add the remaining ingredients. Cover with foil.

② Transfer to the steamer, cover with a lid and steam for 45 minutes until the lentils and vegetables are tender and most of the liquid is absorbed. Discard the bay leaf and serve, garnished with the chopped parsley.

PREPARATION AND COOKING TIME: 55 MINUTES

Carrot and courgette ribbons with mustard seeds

SERVES 4

2 courgettes (zucchini)
2 carrots
A pinch of salt
15 ml/1 tbsp black mustard seeds
25 g/1 oz/2 tbsp butter or margarine

① Shave the courgettes and carrots into ribbons with a potato peeler.

② Toss with the salt and mustard seeds, then place on a large piece of foil and dot with the butter or margarine.

③ Wrap loosely in the foil and place in a steamer. Cover with a lid and steam for 10 minutes until the vegetables are just cooked but still have some 'bite'. Serve hot.

PREPARATION AND COOKING TIME: 20 MINUTES

Warm Russian salad
SERVES 4

This is perfect with cold meats or steamed oily fish such as mackerel, herring or salmon. If you prefer to eat it cold, leave the vegetables to cool completely before adding to the dressing.

½ small swede (rutabaga), cut into small dice
1 large potato, cut into small dice
1 large carrot, cut into small dice
1 turnip, cut into small dice
Salt and freshly ground black pepper
45 ml/3 tbsp mayonnaise
45 ml/3 tbsp crème fraîche
15 ml/1 tbsp snipped fresh chives, for garnishing

① Spread the vegetables out in a steamer container. Sprinkle with salt. Transfer to a steamer, cover with a lid and steam for 20 minutes until really tender.

② Mix the mayonnaise with the crème fraîche and season with a little salt and pepper. Add the vegetables and toss to coat completely.

③ Turn into a serving dish and sprinkle with the chives. Serve while still warm.

PREPARATION AND COOKING TIME: 30 MINUTES

Sweet and sour medley

SERVES 4

This is particularly good served with grilled (broiled) pork chops or chicken portions. You can also serve it as a main course with rice – add a drained can of soya beans for extra protein.

4 spring onions (scallions), cut into short lengths
2 carrots, cut into matchsticks
1/4 cucumber, cut into matchsticks
2 celery sticks, cut into matchsticks
1 red (bell) pepper, cut into thin strips
10 ml/2 tsp cornflour (cornstarch)
30 ml/2 tbsp white wine vinegar
30 ml/2 tbsp water
A good pinch of ground ginger
150 ml/1/4 pt/2/3 cup chicken or vegetable stock, made with 1/2 stock cube
15 ml/1 tbsp light brown sugar
30 ml/2 tbsp soy sauce

① Put all the vegetables in an even layer in a shallow heatproof dish that will fit in or over a steamer or in the rice bowl of an electric steamer.

② Blend the cornflour with the vinegar and water, then stir in the remaining ingredients. Pour over the vegetables and cover with foil.

③ Transfer to a steamer, cover with a lid and steam for 15 minutes. Stir well, re-cover and steam for a further 15 minutes until the vegetables are just cooked but still have some 'bite'.

④ Stir well and serve hot.

PREPARATION AND COOKING TIME: 45 MINUTES

Mixed mushrooms with wine and garlic
SERVES 4

This is delicious as a starter but can also be served as an accompaniment to plain grilled (broiled) or steamed meat, chicken or fish.

225 g/8 oz mixed mushrooms such as oyster, chestnut, shiitake, morel, button, etc.
25 g/1 oz/2 tbsp butter or margarine
1 garlic clove, crushed
90 ml/6 tbsp dry white wine
Salt and freshly ground black pepper
90 ml/6 tbsp single (light) cream
15 ml/1 tbsp chopped fresh parsley
To serve:
French bread

① Trim and cut the mushrooms into thick slices.

② Melt the butter or margarine in a shallow dish in a steamer or in the rice bowl of an electric steamer. Stir in the garlic.

③ Add the mushrooms and toss gently. Pour over the wine and season with salt and pepper. Cover the dish with foil, transfer to the steamer, then cover with a lid and steam for 25 minutes.

④ Stir in the cream. Taste and re-season if necessary. Leave in the steamer, uncovered, for 2 minutes to heat through without boiling at all.

⑤ Spoon into warm individual dishes. Sprinkle with the parsley and serve with lots of French bread to mop up the juices.

PREPARATION AND COOKING TIME: ABOUT 35 MINUTES

Fruit

Steaming is an excellent way of cooking fruit. It helps to preserve the colours and nutrients and, because it is such a gentle method, it helps all fruits to keep their shape (unless you overcook them of course!)

Steaming fresh fruit

Prepare fruit in the same way as for poaching or baking. Put in an even layer in a dish that will fit in the steamer.

You can steam sweet fruit with no added sweetener or liquid. The juices will run naturally as the fruit cooks. You can always add sugar or some other sweetener at the end of cooking if necessary. If you want to steam in sugar syrup, as a guide, use about 100 g/4 oz/½ cup sugar and 300 ml/½ pt/1¼ cups water for each 450 g/1 lb fruit. If the fruit is very sharp, you can always sweeten again after cooking. Alternatively, add other liquid, like wine or fruit juice, if required.

Cover the dish with foil and steam until tender. The time will depend on the quantity and the ripeness of the fruit. Ripe soft fruits – such as raspberries – will be ready after about 5 minutes as they are already soft, but for hard fruits – such as rhubarb and apples – you should allow 10–20 minutes per 450 g/1 lb.

You can use this method to steam soft fruits for a summer pudding: use 700 g/1½ lb fruit with 100 g/4 oz/½ cup of caster (superfine) sugar and 60 ml/4 tbsp of water. Remove the crusts from 5 slices of white bread, dip them in the juice, then use to line a 1 litre/1¾ pt/4¼ cup pudding basin, dipped-sides out. Fill with the fruit, then top with 2 more slices. Cover and weigh down with cans on top, then chill for 24 hours before turning out.

Spiced honey and red wine pears with lime cream

SERVES 4

150 ml/'/₄ pt/²/₃ cup red wine
45 ml/3 tbsp clear honey
A piece of cinnamon stick
2 cloves
4 ripe pears
1 lime
150 ml/'/₄ pt/²/₃ cup crème fraîche
30 ml/2 tbsp icing (confectioners') sugar

① Mix the wine and honey either in a bowl over a pan of simmering water or in the rice bowl of an electric steamer. Add the cinnamon and cloves. Cover and heat while you peel the pears.

② Put the pears in the hot wine, and turn over in the liquid. Cover with foil, then a lid and steam for 10 minutes. Carefully turn the fruit over, re-cover and steam for a further 5 minutes.

③ Meanwhile, finely grate the rind from the lime and stir into the crème fraîche with 5 ml/1 tsp of the juice and all the icing sugar.

④ Discard the cinnamon stick and cloves. Serve the pears hot, or cool, then chill, before serving with the lime cream.

PREPARATION AND COOKING TIME: 20 MINUTES
PLUS CHILLING, IF REQUIRED

Blackberry-stuffed apples
SERVES 4

You can use other soft fruits for the stuffing, but blackberries are natural partners for apples. You can buy excellent ready-made custard in cartons, or, if you prefer, use my recipe on page 150.

4 even-sized cooking (tart) apples, cored but not peeled
75 g/3 oz fresh blackberries
60 ml/4 tbsp golden (light corn) syrup
4 digestive biscuits (graham crackers), crushed
30 ml/2 tbsp water
To serve:
Custard

① With a sharp knife, score a line just through the skin round the middle of each apple to prevent the skins bursting during steaming.

② Stand the fruit in a shallow dish that will fit in or over a steamer.

③ Mix half the blackberries with 30 ml/2 tbsp of the syrup and the biscuit crumbs. Pack tightly into the centres of the apples. Put the remaining blackberries around the apples, then spoon the remaining syrup over the top of the apples.

④ Add the water to the dish. Transfer to the steamer, cover with a lid and steam for 20 minutes until cooked through but the apples still hold their shape.

⑤ Transfer the apples to warm plates. Lift the remaining blackberries out of the dish with a draining spoon and put on the plates with the apples. Spoon the syrupy blackberry juices over the apples and serve with custard.

PREPARATION AND COOKING TIME: 30 MINUTES

Strawberry, pear and kiwi kebabs with ginger and lemon sauce

SERVES 4

These are also good with drained canned lychees or pineapple chunks instead of pears. You can use bought lemon curd or try my recipe on page 152.

16 large strawberries, hulled
1 pear, peeled, cored and cut into 8 chunks
1 kiwi fruit, peeled and cut into 8 chunks
1 piece of stem ginger in syrup, finely chopped
30 ml/2 tbsp ginger syrup, from the jar
60 ml/4 tbsp lemon curd
To serve:
Crème fraîche

1. Cut four wooden skewers in half. Thread a strawberry, then a piece of kiwi fruit, then a piece of pear and finally another strawberry on each stick.

2. Mix the remaining ingredients in a shallow dish that will fit in or over a steamer or in the rice bowl of an electric steamer.

3. Lay the kebabs in the dish and spoon the sauce over.

4. Transfer to the steamer, cover tightly with a lid and steam for 10 minutes.

5. Lift the kebabs on to warm plates. Spoon the sauce over and serve straight away with a dollop of crème fraîche on the side.

PREPARATION AND COOKING TIME: 15 MINUTES

Mango in rum with kiwi coulis

SERVES 4

2 large mangoes
1 lime
25 g/1 oz/ 2 tbsp caster (superfine) sugar
30 ml/2 tbsp white rum
2 kiwi fruit
To serve:
Crème fraîche

① Peel the mangoes. Slice off the fruit from the stones (pits). Thinly pare the rind from the lime and cut into thin shreds. Squeeze the juice.

② Mix the juice with the sugar and rum in a shallow dish that will fit in or over a steamer. Add the mango slices. Put the lime rind in a separate little pile to one side of the fruit.

③ Cover with foil and steam for 8 minutes. Leave to cool, then chill.

④ Remove the lime rind and reserve. Pour off the mango liquid. Purée the kiwi fruit in a blender or food processor with the mango liquid.

⑤ Spoon the kiwi purée on to four dessert plates and spread out. Arrange the mango slices attractively on top and scatter the lime rind over. Serve with crème fraîche.

PREPARATION AND COOKING TIME: 15 MINUTES PLUS CHILLING

Banana and passion fruit pudding

SERVES 4

2 bananas, thickly sliced
1 passion fruit
Finely grated rind and juice of 1 orange
300 ml/½ pt/1¼ cups thick vanilla yoghurt
1 egg
45 ml/3 tbsp soft dark brown sugar

① Place the slices of banana in a shallow heatproof dish that will fit in or over a steamer. Halve the passion fruit, scoop out the seeds and add to the bananas. Add the orange rind and juice and stir gently to mix.

② Whisk the yoghurt and egg together and spoon on top.

③ Transfer to the steamer, cover with a lid and steam for 30 minutes until the top has set.

④ Remove from the steamer, sprinkle liberally with the sugar. Leave until cool, then chill before serving.

PREPARATION AND COOKING TIME: 40 MINUTES PLUS CHILLING

Pineapple and coconut boats
SERVES 4

1 small pineapple, cut into quarters
2 egg whites
100 g/4 oz/½ cup caster (superfine) sugar
Finely grated rind of ½ lemon
75 g/3 oz/¾ cup desiccated (shredded) coconut
4 small sprigs of fresh mint, for decorating
To serve:
Golden Brandy Sauce (see page 153)

① Cut the skin in one piece off each pineapple quarter, then cut out any woody core. Chop the fruit and drain on kitchen paper (paper towels). Put the four pineapple skins on foil in a steamer tier. Spoon the fruit back on the skins.

② Put the egg whites in a bowl and whisk until stiff. Whisk in the sugar until glossy and peaking. Fold in the lemon rind and coconut.

③ Pile on to the pineapple. Transfer to the steamer, cover with a lid and steam for 10 minutes until the topping is set.

④ Transfer to warm plates. Spoon the Golden Brandy Sauce around and decorate each with a sprig of mint.

PREPARATION AND COOKING TIME: 20 MINUTES

Fresh peaches and cream fondue

SERVES 4

4 ripe peaches, peeled, halved and stoned (pitted)
15 ml/1 tbsp icing (confectioners') sugar
10 ml/2 tsp lemon juice
5 ml/1 tsp arrowroot
30 ml/2 tbsp peach liqueur or brandy
30 ml/2 tbsp double (heavy) cream
To serve:
Sponge (lady) fingers

① Purée the peaches in a blender or food processor.

② Blend the icing sugar with the lemon juice, arrowroot and liqueur or brandy in a bowl over a pan of simmering water, or in a double saucepan, or in the rice bowl of an electric steamer. Stir in the peach purée.

③ Cook, stirring, for 15 minutes until piping hot and slightly thickened. Pour into small pots.

④ Add a little cream to each and swirl with a teaspoon to give a marbled effect. Serve straight away with sponge fingers to dip in.

PREPARATION AND COOKING TIME: 20 MINUTES

Sherried strawberry compôte
SERVED 4

Use ripe, sweet strawberries for this recipe. If the fruit is not completely ripe, sweeten the juice to taste with a little sugar after steaming.

200 ml/7 fl oz/scant 1 cup apple juice
45 ml/3 tbsp strawberry jam (conserve)
10 ml/2 tsp lemon juice
45 ml/3 tbsp medium-dry sherry
450 g/1 lb even-sized strawberries, hulled
To serve:
Whipped cream or vanilla ice cream

① Mix the juice, jam, lemon juice and sherry in a bowl that will fit in or over a steamer or in the rice bowl of an electric steamer. Add the strawberries.

② Cover the dish with foil, then transfer to the steamer, cover with a lid and steam for 10–15 minutes. Stir gently after 10 minutes. You will be able to see whether the fruit is nearly cooked or will take the extra 5 minutes.

③ Turn into a serving dish, if necessary, and serve warm or cold with whipped cream or ice cream.

PREPARATION AND COOKING TIME: 15–20 MINUTES

Nectarines stuffed with mincemeat
SERVES 4

You can steam the sabayon in a bowl set in or over the steamer or in the rice bowl of an electric steamer at the same time as the fruit.

4 nectarines
120 ml/8 tbsp mincemeat
15 g/¹/₂ oz/1 tbsp butter (optional)
To serve:
Brandy Sabayon (see page 151) and shortbread fingers

① Cut the nectarines into halves and remove the stones (pits).

② Line a steamer container with foil to catch the juice. Put the fruit in the container, cut sides up, and put a spoonful of mincemeat in each cavity. Dot the tops with the butter, if using.

③ Transfer to the steamer, cover with a lid and steam for 10–15 minutes – the time will vary according to how ripe the fruit is.

④ Carefully lift out the fruit and place in shallow serving dishes. Spoon the juices over and serve with Brandy Sabayon and shortbread fingers.

PREPARATION AND COOKING TIME: 15–20 MINUTES

Victoria pudding
SERVES 4

If using custard, you can either buy it ready-made or use my recipe on page 150.

450 g/1 lb Victoria plums, halved and stoned (pitted)
50 g/2 oz/¼ cup caster (superfine) sugar
10 ml/2 tsp cornflour (cornstarch)
100 g/4 oz/½ cup soft tub margarine
100 g/4 oz/1 cup soft dark brown sugar
100 g/4 oz/1 cup self-raising (self-rising) flour
5 ml/1 tsp baking powder
2 eggs
15 ml/1 tbsp icing (confectioners') sugar, for decorating
To serve:
Cream or custard

① Put the plums in the base of a greased 1.2 litre/2 pt/5 cup heatproof dish that will fit in a steamer. Sprinkle with the caster sugar and cornflour. Stir to mix thoroughly, then spread out again.

② Put all the remaining ingredients in a bowl and beat with a wooden spoon until blended. Alternatively, place in a food processor and run the machine briefly to mix.

③ Spoon the mixture over the plums. Cover with greased foil with a pleat in the centre to allow for rising. Twist and fold under the rim to secure or tie with string.

④ Transfer to the steamer, cover with a lid and steam for 1½ hours until cooked through and spongy on top.

⑤ Dust the top with sifted icing sugar and serve with cream or custard.

PREPARATION AND COOKING TIME: 1¾ HOURS

Cherry and chocolate chip upside-down pudding
SERVES 4

75 g/3 oz/³/₄ cup self-raising (self-rising) flour
25 g/1 oz/¹/₄ cup cocoa (unsweetened chocolate) powder
5 ml/1 tsp baking powder
100 g/4 oz/¹/₂ cup caster (superfine) sugar
100 g/4 oz/¹/₂ cup softened butter or margarine, plus
   extra for greasing
2.5 ml/¹/₂ tsp vanilla essence (extract)
50 g/2 oz/¹/₂ cup plain (semi-sweet) chocolate chips
400 g/14 oz/1 large can of cherry pie filling
To serve:
Cream

① Thoroughly grease a 20 cm/8 in soufflé dish with butter or margarine.

② Put all the ingredients except the cherry pie filling in a bowl and beat well until blended.

③ Spoon the pie filling into the prepared dish and spread out evenly. Spoon the chocolate mixture over to cover the cherries completely.

④ Cover the dish with well-greased foil with a pleat in the middle to allow for rising. Twist and fold under the rim to secure.

⑤ Transfer to a steamer, cover with a lid and steam for 1¹/₂ hours.

⑥ Loosen the edge with a round-bladed knife, then turn the pudding out on to a warm serving plate. The cherries will ooze down the sides like a sauce. Serve hot with cream.

PREPARATION AND COOKING TIME: 1 HOUR 40 MINUTES

Traditional Recipes

*T*his section is devoted to those hearty, rib-sticking sweet and savoury puddings that we all love (including the most traditional of all, Christmas Pudding). In addition, you'll find galantines and meat rolls – all full of flavour and particularly comforting on chilly winter days.

They're not for weight-watchers or fans of nouvelle cuisine and there's no doubt that you shouldn't indulge in this type of thing too often. But I'm sure you'll agree, they are exceptionally good once in a while!

Steak and kidney pudding

SERVES 4

If you buy ready-prepared mixed steak and kidney, ask for 550 g/1 ¼ lb.

For the suet pastry (paste):
225 g/8 oz/2 cups self-raising (self-rising) flour
2.5 ml/½ tsp salt
100 g/4 oz/1 cup shredded (chopped) beef or vegetable suet
A little cold water
For the filling:
450 g/1 lb lean stewing steak, cubed
100 g/4 oz ox kidney, cored and cut into bite-sized pieces
15 g/½ oz/2 tbsp plain (all-purpose) flour
Freshly ground black pepper
1 large onion, thinly sliced
1 potato, diced
150 ml/¼ pt/⅔ cup beef stock, made with ½ stock cube
To serve:
Gravy, carrots, cabbage and mustard

① To make the pastry, sift the flour and salt into a bowl. Stir in the suet and mix with enough cold water to form a soft but not sticky dough.

② Knead gently on a lightly floured surface. Cut off a quarter of the dough (this will make a lid), roll out the remainder and use to line a greased 1.2 litre/2 pt/5 cup pudding basin.

③ Mix the beef and kidney with the plain flour and some salt and pepper. Layer with the sliced onion and potato in the basin. Add the stock.

④ Brush the edges of the pastry with a little water. Roll out the reserved pastry to a round the size of the top of the basin and place on top. Press the edges well together to seal. Cover with a double thickness of greased greaseproof (waxed) paper or foil with a pleat in the middle to allow for rising. Twist and fold under the rim of the basin to secure or tie with string. Transfer to a steamer, cover with a lid and steam for 4 hours.

⑤ Serve straight from the basin or turn out on to a warm serving dish, with extra gravy, carrots and cabbage and mustard.

PREPARATION AND COOKING TIME: 4½ HOURS

Steak and mushroom pudding

Make in the same way, substituting small button mushrooms for the kidney.

Steak and ale pudding

Make in the same way, omitting the kidney and adding a large, thinly sliced carrot to the mixture. Moisten with brown ale instead of the stock.

Bacon, corn, mustard and herb dome
SERVES 4–5

For the filling:
450 g/1 lb unsmoked bacon joint
15 g/¹⁄₂ oz/1 tbsp butter or margarine
**295 g/10¹⁄₂ oz/1 medium can of condensed cream of
  celery soup**
200 g/7 oz/1 small can of sweetcorn (corn), drained
Freshly ground black pepper
For the pastry (paste):
225 g/8 oz/2 cups self-raising (self-rising) flour
2.5 ml/¹⁄₂ tsp salt
5 ml/1 tsp mustard powder
100 g/4 oz/1 cup shredded (chopped) beef or vegetable suet
5 ml/1 tsp dried mixed herbs
30 ml/2 tbsp chopped fresh parsley
Cold water, to mix
To serve:
French (green) beans

① Dice the bacon, discarding any rind and fat. If you think the
   meat may be salty, soak it in cold water for 2–3 hours, then
   drain thoroughly.

② Melt the butter or margarine in a saucepan. Add the meat
   and fry (sauté), stirring, for 2 minutes. Remove from the
   heat. Stir in the soup and sweetcorn and season with
   pepper.

③ To make the pastry, sift the flour, salt and mustard powder
   into a bowl. Stir in the suet, mixed herbs and parsley and
   mix with enough water to form a soft but not sticky dough.
   Knead gently on a lightly floured surface.

④ Cut off a quarter of the dough and reserve (for a lid), then
   roll out the remainder and use to line a greased 1.2 litre/
   2 pt/5 cup pudding basin.

⑤ Turn the filling into the basin. Brush the edges with water. Roll out the reserved dough to a round the size of the top of the basin and press into position.

⑥ Cover with a double thickness of greased greaseproof (waxed) paper or foil with a pleat in the middle to allow for rising. Twist and fold under the rim of the basin to secure or tie with string.

⑦ Transfer to a steamer, cover with a lid and steam for 2½ hours.

⑧ Serve straight from the basin with French beans.

PREPARATION AND COOKING TIME: 3 HOURS

Chicken galantine
SERVES 8

Serve any leftovers cold the next day with salad or use as a filling for sandwiches or baguettes. If your loaf is too large to fit in a steamer, use a bain marie (see page 7).

700 g/1½ lb minced (ground) chicken
100 g/4 oz cooked ham, very finely chopped
225 g/8 oz pork sausagemeat
1 onion, very finely chopped
100 g/4 oz/2 cups fresh white breadcrumbs
5 ml/1 tsp dried oregano
Salt and freshly ground black pepper
A little cayenne
1 large egg, beaten
For the sauce:
1 bunch of spring onions (scallions), chopped
15 g/1 oz/1 tbsp butter or margarine
400 g/14 oz/1 large can of chopped tomatoes
15 ml/1 tbsp tomato purée (paste)
A good pinch of caster (superfine) sugar
To serve:
New potatoes and courgettes (zucchini)

① Mix all the ingredients for the galantine thoroughly together in a large bowl (you may find it best to mix with your hands), seasoning well.

② Turn into a greased 900 g/2 lb loaf tin (pan) and press down well. Cover tightly with foil, twisting and folding under the rim of the tin to secure.

③ Transfer to a steamer, cover with a lid and steam for 2 hours.

④ Meanwhile, make the sauce. Fry (sauté) the spring onions in the butter or margarine for 2 minutes, stirring all the time. Add the tomatoes, tomato purée and sugar. Bring to the boil, reduce the heat and simmer for 5 minutes until pulpy. Season the sauce with salt, pepper and cayenne to taste.

⑤ Remove the galantine from the pan and leave to stand for 5 minutes. Turn out on to a warm serving dish and serve sliced with the spicy tomato sauce, new potatoes and courgettes.

PREPARATION AND COOKING TIME: 2 HOURS 10 MINUTES

Beef galantine

Prepare in exactly the same way, using minced (ground) beef and sausagemeat. Flavour with dried mixed herbs instead of oregano. Serve with canned creamed mushrooms instead of the tomato sauce for a change.

Pork galantine

Prepare in exactly the same way, using minced (ground) pork instead of chicken and finely chopped streaky bacon instead of ham. Flavour with dried sage instead of oregano.

Stuffed pork roll

SERVES 4–6

900 g/2 lb piece of lean belly pork
Salt and freshly ground black pepper
2.5 ml/½ tsp ground allspice
100 g/4 oz/2 cups fresh white breadcrumbs
1 onion, finely chopped
15 ml/1 tbsp chopped fresh sage
15 ml/1 tbsp chopped fresh parsley
1 egg, beaten
60 ml/4 tbsp dried breadcrumbs
To serve:
Crusty bread, pickles and a mixed salad

① Place the meat, rind-side down, on a board and cut away all the bones.

② Mix 2.5 ml/½ tsp salt with a good grinding of pepper and the allspice and rub all over the meat.

③ Mix together the fresh breadcrumbs, onion, sage and parsley. Season with a little more salt and pepper and mix with the beaten egg to bind.

④ Spread all over the meat, to within 1 cm/½ in of the edges. Roll up and tie securely with string.

⑤ Wrap tightly in foil, twisting the ends to seal thoroughly.

⑥ Transfer to a steamer, cover and steam for 4 hours. Remove from the steamer and leave until cold.

⑦ Remove the string and rind and roll in the dried breadcrumbs to coat. Cut into slices before serving with crusty bread, pickles and a mixed salad.

PREPARATION AND COOKING TIME: 4 HOURS 25 MINUTES PLUS COOLING

Spotted dick

SERVES 4–6

*You can use half currants and half sultanas (golden raisins),
if you prefer.*

---

100 g/4 oz/1 cup plain (all-purpose) flour
10 ml/2 tsp baking powder
100 g/4 oz/2 cups fresh white breadcrumbs
100 g/4 oz/1 cup chopped (shredded) beef or vegetable suet
75 g/3 oz/⅓ cup caster (superfine) sugar
100 g/4 oz/²/₃ cup currants
2 eggs, beaten
75 ml/5 tbsp milk
For the syrup sauce:
90 ml/6 tbsp golden (light corn) syrup
30 ml/2 tbsp lemon juice
To serve:
Custard (see page 150) or cream

---

① Sift the flour and baking powder into a bowl.

② Stir in the breadcrumbs, suet, sugar and currants.

③ Mix with the eggs and enough milk to form a soft, dropping consistency. Shape into a roll on a double thickness of greased, greaseproof (waxed) paper or foil. Wrap up loosely and tie the ends with twist ties or string.

④ Transfer to a steamer, cover and steam for 2½ hours.

⑤ Meanwhile, make the sauce. Put the syrup and lemon juice in a small bowl. Place in a tier above the pudding in the steamer and steam for the last 5 minutes until hot, runny and blended.

⑥ Unwrap the pudding on to a warm serving dish. Spoon a little syrup sauce over, then slice and serve with the remaining sauce and custard or cream.

PREPARATION AND COOKING TIME: 2 HOURS 45 MINUTES

Jam roly poly with jam sauce

SERVES 4

A little butter or margarine, for greasing
175 g/6 oz/1½ cups self-raising (self-rising) flour
A pinch of salt
75 g/3 oz/¾ cup shredded (chopped) beef or vegetable suet
1 egg, beaten
60 ml/4 tbsp milk
120 ml/8 tbsp raspberry jam (conserve)
A little extra milk, for brushing
30 ml/2 tbsp caster (superfine) sugar
Finely grated rind and juice of ½ lemon
75 ml/5 tbsp water
A little sifted icing (confectioners') sugar, for decorating
To serve:
Custard (see page 150)

① Grease the shiny side of a 30 cm/12 in square of foil with the butter or margarine.

② Sift the flour and salt into a bowl and stir in the suet. Add the beaten egg and enough of the milk to form a soft but not sticky dough. Knead gently on a lightly floured surface. Roll out to a rectangle about 20 x 25 cm/8 x 10 in.

③ Spread half the jam over, leaving a border about 1 cm/½ in wide all round. Brush the border with a little milk. Roll up, starting at a short end. Place on the greased foil and wrap loosely to allow for expansion. Make sure the edges are sealed well to prevent moisture getting into the parcel.

④ Transfer to a steamer, cover with a lid and steam for 1½ hours.

⑤ Heat the remaining jam with the caster sugar, lemon rind and juice and the water in a small saucepan, stirring until smooth.

⑥ Unwrap the pudding and place on a warm serving dish. Dust with the sifted icing sugar and serve with the hot jam sauce and custard.

PREPARATION AND COOKING TIME: 1 HOUR 45 MINUTES

Christmas pudding
SERVES 8

Make at least 6 weeks before Christmas, if possible, to allow the flavours to develop.

100 g/4 oz/1 cup plain (all-purpose) flour
100 g/4 oz/2 cups fresh white breadcrumbs
1.5 ml/¼ tsp salt
5 ml/1 tsp mixed (apple-pie) spice
100 g/4 oz/1 cup shredded (chopped) beef or vegetable suet
175 g/6 oz/¾ cup soft dark brown sugar
450 g/1 lb/2⅔ cups mixed dried fruit (fruit cake mix)
1 small carrot, grated
1 small eating (dessert) or cooking (tart) apple, grated
1 large egg, beaten
100 ml/3½ fl oz/scant ½ cup stout or brown ale
A little butter or margarine, for greasing
To serve:
Brandy Sabayon (see page 151) and cream

① Mix all the ingredients except the eggs and stout in a large bowl. When thoroughly blended, stir in the eggs and stout to form a moist mixture. Cover with a clean cloth and leave to stand for 24 hours.

② Grease a 900 ml/1½ pt/3¾ cup pudding basin and line the base with a circle of greased greaseproof (waxed) paper. Turn the mixture into the basin and level the surface.

③ Cover with a circle of greaseproof paper, then an old saucer, rounded side up. Finally cover with a double thickness of foil, twisting and folding under the rim of the basin to secure.

④ Transfer to a steamer, cover with a lid and steam for 6–7 hours until really dark in colour. Cool, then remove the foil and re-cover with clean foil. Store in a cool dark place.

⑤ When ready to serve, steam again for 2½ hours. Serve hot with Brandy Sabayon and cream.

PREPARATION AND COOKING TIME: 6–7 HOURS PLUS STANDING,
THEN 2½ HOURS FINAL COOKING

Mincemeat layer

SERVES 6

This recipe will probably suit those who like mince pies but aren't too keen on Christmas pudding.

45 ml/3 tbsp mincemeat
100 g/4 oz/½ cup soft tub margarine
100 g/4 oz/½ cup caster (superfine) sugar
150 g/5 oz/1¼ cups self-raising (self-rising) flour
5 ml/1 tsp baking powder
25 g/1 oz/¼ cup ground almonds
A few drops of almond essence (extract)
2 eggs
To serve:
Vanilla ice cream

① Place 15 ml/1 tbsp of the mincemeat in the base of a greased 900 ml/1½ pt/3¾ cup pudding basin.

② Put all the remaining ingredients except the rest of the mincemeat in a large mixing bowl and beat well until smooth. Spoon half the sponge mixture into the pudding basin. Spread the reserved mincemeat over, then top with the remaining sponge mixture.

③ Cover with a double thickness of greased greaseproof (waxed) paper or foil with a pleat in the centre to allow for rising. Twist and fold under the rim of the basin to secure or tie with string.

④ Transfer to a steamer, cover with a lid and steam for 2 hours.

⑤ Turn out and serve warm with ice cream.

PREPARATION AND COOKING TIME: 2 HOURS 10 MINUTES

Syrup sponge pudding
SERVES 6

You can use jam (conserve) instead of syrup, if you prefer.

A little butter or margarine, for greasing
45 ml/3 tbsp golden (light corn) syrup
100 g/4 oz/½ cup soft tub margarine
100 g/4 oz/½ cup caster (superfine) sugar
2 eggs
175 g/6 oz/1½ cups self-raising (self-rising) flour
5 ml/1 tsp baking powder
30 ml/2 tbsp milk
To serve:
Extra syrup and custard (see page 150)

① Grease a 1.2 litre/2 pt/5 cup pudding basin with a little butter or margarine. Put the golden syrup in the base.

② Put the margarine, sugar, eggs, flour and baking powder in a large mixing bowl and beat well until smooth. Spoon into the basin and level the surface.

③ Cover with a double thickness of greased greaseproof (waxed) paper or foil with a pleat in the centre to allow for rising. Twist and fold under the rim of the basin to secure or tie with string. Transfer to a steamer, cover with a lid and steam for 2 hours.

④ Turn out and serve with extra golden syrup and cream.

PREPARATION AND COOKING TIME: 2 HOURS 10 MINUTES

Syrup and ginger pudding
Prepare in the same way, adding 7.5 ml/1½ tsp ground ginger to the sponge mixture.

Syrup and lemon pudding
Prepare in the same way, adding the grated rind and juice of ½ lemon to the mixture and omitting 15 ml/1 tbsp of the milk.

Real treacle pudding
SERVES 6

175 g/6 oz/1½ cups plain (all-purpose) flour
2.5 ml/½ tsp ground ginger
175 g/6 oz/3 cups fresh white breadcrumbs
100 g/4 oz/1 cup shredded (chopped) beef or vegetable suet
1 egg, beaten
175 g/6 oz/½ cup black treacle (molasses)
45 ml/3 tbsp milk
2.5 ml/½ tsp bicarbonate of soda (baking soda)
A little butter or margarine, for greasing
To serve:
Whipped cream

① Sift the flour and ginger into a bowl. Stir in the breadcrumbs and suet.

② Add the beaten egg. Warm the treacle and milk in a saucepan, then stir in the bicarbonate of soda. Mix with the dry ingredients to form a soft, dropping consistency.

③ Grease a 1.25 litre/2¼ pt/5½ cup pudding basin with butter or margarine. Turn the mixture into the basin. Cover with a double thickness of greased greaseproof (waxed) paper or foil with a pleat in the centre to allow for rising. Twist and fold under the rim of the basin to secure or tie with string.

④ Transfer to a steamer, cover with a lid and steam for 2½ hours. Turn out and serve with whipped cream.

PREPARATION AND COOKING TIME: 2 HOURS 40 MINUTES

Sussex pond pudding
SERVES 6

This can be made with a whole lemon in the centre, but I prefer this version!

---

225 g/8 oz/2 cups self-raising (self-rising) flour
A pinch of salt
100 g/4 oz/1 cup shredded (chopped) beef or vegetable suet
100 g/4 oz/²/₃ cup currants
150 g/5 oz/²/₃ cup soft light brown sugar
Grated rind and juice of 1 lemon
Cold water, to mix
100 g/4 oz/¹/₂ cup butter, plus a little for greasing
To serve:
Cream

---

① Sift the flour and salt into a bowl. Add the suet, currants and 25 g/1 oz/2 tbsp of the sugar. Mix with the lemon juice and enough water to form a soft but not sticky dough. Knead gently on a lightly floured surface.

② Cut off a quarter of the dough and roll out to a round the size of the top of the basin to use as a 'lid'. Roll out the remaining dough and use to line a greased 900 ml/1¹/₂ pt/ 3³/₄ cup pudding basin.

③ Beat the remaining sugar, the lemon rind and butter together until smooth. Spoon into the basin, then brush the edges of the dough with water and cover with the 'lid'. Press the edges well together to seal.

④ Cover with a double thickness of greased greaseproof (waxed) paper or foil with a pleat in the middle to allow for rising. Twist and fold under the rim of the basin to secure or tie with string.

⑤ Transfer to a steamer, cover with a lid and steam for 2¹/₂ hours.

⑥ Turn out and serve with cream.

PREPARATION AND COOKING TIME: 2¾ HOURS

Apple dumpling
SERVES 4–6

225 g/8 oz/2 cups plain (all-purpose) flour
A pinch of salt
15 ml/1 tbsp baking powder
75 g/3 oz/¾ cup shredded (chopped) beef or vegetable suet
Cold water, to mix
700 g/1½ lb cooking (tart) apples, peeled, cored and sliced
50 g/2 oz/¼ cup granulated sugar
1.5 ml/¼ tsp ground cloves
To serve:
Clotted cream (see page 155)

① Sift the flour, salt and baking powder into a bowl. Stir in the suet and mix with enough cold water to form a soft but not sticky dough. Knead gently on a lightly floured surface.

② Cut off a quarter of the dough. Roll out to the size of the top of the basin and reserve for a 'lid'. Roll out the remaining dough and use to line a greased 900 ml/1½ pt/ 3¾ cup pudding basin.

③ Mix the apples, sugar and cloves together and use to fill the basin. Add 15 ml/1 tbsp cold water. Dampen the dough edges with a little more water and place the 'lid' in position. Press the edges well together to seal.

④ Cover with a double thickness of greased, greaseproof (waxed) paper or foil with a pleat in the centre to allow for rising. Twist and fold under the rim of the basin to secure or tie with string.

⑤ Transfer to a steamer, cover with a lid and steam for 2½–3 hours.

⑥ Remove the greaseproof paper or foil. Tie a clean napkin around the basin and serve straight from the basin with clotted cream.

PREPARATION AND COOKING TIME: 2¾–3¼ HOURS

Brown betty
SERVES 6

50 g/2 oz/¼ cup butter or margarine, plus a little
   for greasing
100 g/4 oz/2 cups fresh wholemeal breadcrumbs
2.5 ml/½ tsp ground cinnamon
25 g/1 oz/2 tbsp soft light brown sugar
450 g/1 lb cooking (tart) apples, thinly sliced
50 g/2 oz/⅓ cup sultanas (golden raisins)
30 ml/2 tbsp golden (light corn) syrup
15 ml/1 tbsp water
To serve:
Custard (see page 150)

① Grease a 900 ml/1½ pt/3¾ cup pudding basin. Add a few
   of the breadcrumbs and tilt the basin so that they coat the
   whole inside surface.

② Mix the cinnamon and sugar together. Put layers of apple,
   breadcrumbs, sultanas and the cinnamon and sugar
   mixture in the basin. Dot with the butter or margarine.

③ Blend the syrup and water and pour over. Cover with a
   double thickness of foil or greaseproof (waxed) paper. Twist
   and fold under the rim of the basin to secure, or tie with
   string.

④ Transfer to a steamer, cover with a lid and steam for
   2 hours.

⑤ Serve warm with custard.

PREPARATION AND COOKING TIME: 2½ HOURS

Figgy pudding
SERVES 6

This is another traditional pudding to serve at Christmas time, served with Golden Brandy Sauce (see page 153).

225 g/8 oz/1⅓ cups dried figs, chopped
100 g/4 oz/1 cup shredded (chopped) beef or vegetable suet
100 g/4 oz/2 cups fresh wholemeal breadcrumbs
100 g/4 oz/2 cups fresh white breadcrumbs
25 g/1 oz/2 tbsp caster (superfine) sugar
2 eggs, beaten
150 ml/¼ pt/⅔ cup milk
A little butter or margarine, for greasing
To serve:
Custard (see page 150) and cream

① Mix the figs, suet, breadcrumbs and sugar in a bowl.

② Add the beaten eggs and milk and mix to form a soft, dropping consistency.

③ Grease a 1.2 litre/2 pt/5 cup pudding basin. Turn the mixture into the basin, then cover with a double thickness of greased greaseproof (waxed) paper or foil with a pleat in the centre to allow for rising. Twist and fold under the rim of the basin to secure or tie with string.

④ Transfer to a steamer, cover with a lid and steam for 4 hours.

⑤ Turn out and serve with custard and cream.

PREPARATION AND COOKING TIME: 4 HOURS 10 MINUTES

Chocolate pudding with built-in sauce

SERVES 4–6

75 g/3 oz/³/₄ cup self-raising (self-rising) flour
5 ml/1 tsp baking powder
50 g/2 oz/¹/₂ cup cocoa (unsweetened chocolate) powder
50 g/2 oz/¹/₄ cup soft tub margarine
25 g/1 oz/2 tbsp caster (superfine) sugar
1 egg, beaten
15 ml/1 tbsp milk
A little butter or margarine, for greasing
10 ml/2 tsp cornflour (cornstarch)
15 g/¹/₂ oz/1 tbsp soft light brown sugar
150 ml/¹/₄ pt/²/₃ cup water
To serve:
Cream

① Sift the flour, baking powder and half the cocoa powder into a bowl.

② Add 40 g/1¹/₂ oz/3 tbsp of the margarine, the caster sugar, egg and milk and beat together until smooth.

③ Grease a 900 ml/1¹/₂ pt/3³/₄ cup pudding basin, then turn the mixture into the basin.

④ Put the remaining cocoa, the cornflour and brown sugar in a saucepan. Blend in the water, then add the remaining margarine. Bring to the boil, stirring until thickened. Pour over the pudding.

⑤ Cover with a double thickness of greased foil with a pleat in the middle to allow for rising. Twist and fold under the rim to secure, or tie with string.

⑥ Transfer to a steamer, cover with a lid and steam for 1¹/₄ hours.

⑦ Loosen the edge with a round-bladed knife, then turn out on to a warm, shallow serving dish. The sauce should trickle down the sides. Serve hot with cream.

PREPARATION AND COOKING TIME: 1¹/₂ HOURS

Cabinet pudding
SERVES 4–6

A little butter or margarine, for greasing
A few glacé (candied) cherries, halved
Angelica leaves
6 blanched almonds
50 g/2 oz sponge (lady) fingers, chopped
50 g/2 oz almond macaroons, roughly crushed
300 ml/¹/₂ pt/1 ¹/₄ cups whipping cream
50 g/2 oz/¹/₄ cup caster (superfine) sugar
2 eggs, beaten
2.5 ml/¹/₂ tsp vanilla essence (extract)
75 ml/5 tbsp white rum
To serve:
Rum Custard Sauce (see page 150)

① Grease a 900 ml/1¹/₂ pt/3³/₄ cup mould. Arrange the cherries, cut sides up, angelica leaves and almonds attractively in the base.

② Mix the crushed sponge fingers and macaroons together. Whisk the cream with the sugar, eggs, vanilla and rum until well blended. Stir in the crushed biscuits (cookies).

③ Leave to soak for 15 minutes. Pour into the mould.

④ Cover with a double thickness of greased greaseproof (waxed) paper or foil. Twist and fold under the rim of the basin to secure.

⑤ Transfer to a steamer, cover with a lid and steam for 1 hour until set. Leave to stand for 5 minutes.

⑥ Turn out and serve with Rum Custard Sauce.

PREPARATION AND COOKING TIME: 1¼ HOURS PLUS STANDING

Bread and Cakes

*T*he wonderful thing about cooking breads and cakes in a steamer is that they stay so soft and moist instead of becoming over-baked and dry. Of course, you don't get the crisp brown surface you would with oven bakes, but there are many recipes that are better without that quality.

Warming and reheating

Your steamer can be used to warm bread, pancakes and tortillas. Wrap rolls, pittas, chapattis, naans or small loaves individually in foil, making sure they are covered completely. Pancakes or flour tortillas may be wrapped together in stacks. Place the foil parcels in a steamer, cover with a lid and steam for about 5 minutes until warm through.

Keeping warm

To keep pancakes warm while cooking the remainder, place them on a plate, cover with another plate or a lid and put the plate over a pan of simmering water.

Steamed sesame buns

MAKES 8

These soft, spongy rolls can be cooked in advance, then re-steamed for about 5 minutes to warm through before serving (particularly useful if you want to serve them for breakfast).

275 g/10 oz/2½ cups strong white (bread) flour, plus extra for dusting
1 sachet of easy-blend dried yeast
5 ml/1 tsp caster (superfine) sugar
5 ml/1 tsp salt
15 ml/1 tbsp sunflower oil
150 ml/¼ pt/²/₃ cup hand-hot water
25 g/1 oz/2 tbsp softened butter or margarine
30 ml/2 tbsp toasted sesame seeds

① Mix the flour with the yeast, sugar and salt in a bowl. Add the oil, then stir in enough water to form a soft, but not sticky, dough.

② Knead gently on a lightly floured surface for 5 minutes until smooth and elastic. Alternatively, blend all the ingredients in a food processor and run the machine for 1 minute to knead.

③ Put the dough in a greased polythene bag and leave in a warm place to rise for 1 hour.

④ Knock back (punch down) the dough and knead again briefly.

⑤ Divide into eight pieces and roll into balls. Place each one on a small square of oiled foil. Mash the butter or margarine with the sesame seeds and spread lightly on top of each bun. Place in two tiered steamer containers. Cover the buns loosely with oiled foil, then cover the tiers with their lids or more foil and leave in a warm place to rise for 30 minutes until well risen again.

⑥ Transfer the tiers to a steamer, cover with a lid and steam for 15 minutes or until cooked through. Serve warm.

PREPARATION AND COOKING TIME: 25 MINUTES PLUS RISING

Country black gingerbread
MAKES A 450 G/1 LB LOAF

100 g/4 oz/1 cup wholemeal flour
50 g/2 oz/¹/₂ cup plain (all-purpose) flour
2.5 ml/¹/₂ tsp salt
2.5 ml/¹/₂ tsp ground cinnamon
10 ml/2 tsp ground ginger
5 ml/1 tsp bicarbonate of soda (baking soda)
30 ml/2 tbsp black treacle (molasses)
75 g/3 oz/¹/₃ cup soft dark brown sugar
25 g/1 oz/2 tbsp butter or margarine, plus extra for
  greasing and spreading
250 ml/8 fl oz/1 cup milk
5 ml/1 tsp lemon juice

① Mix the flours, salt, cinnamon, ginger and bicarbonate of soda thoroughly together in a large bowl.

② Warm the treacle, sugar and butter or margarine in a saucepan until the fat melts. Stir in the milk and lemon juice.

③ Pour a little at a time into the flour mixture and mix thoroughly until smooth.

④ Turn into a greased 18 cm/7 in cake tin (pan), base-lined with greased greaseproof (waxed) paper. Cover with greased foil, with a pleat in the middle to allow for rising. Twist and fold under the rim to secure or tie with string.

⑤ Transfer to a steamer, cover with a lid and steam for 1 hour or until springy to the touch and a skewer inserted in the centre comes out clean. Cool slightly, then turn out, remove the paper and leave to cool.

⑥ Serve sliced and buttered.

PREPARATION AND COOKING TIME: 1 HOUR 10 MINUTES

International flat breads

MAKES 6 SMALL BREADS

These are delicious plain and you can flavour them by gently pressing a sprinkling of sesame, fennel, caraway or poppy seeds into them before wrapping and steaming. Alternatively, once browned on one side, turn them over and spread with a little butter flavoured with garlic or herbs.

250 g/9 oz/2¼ cups plain (all-purpose) flour
1.5 ml/¼ tsp salt
2.5 ml/½ tsp baking powder
5 ml/1 tsp easy-blend dried yeast
5 ml/1 tsp caster (superfine) sugar
15 ml/1 tbsp sunflower oil
75 ml/5 tbsp milk
90 ml/6 tbsp plain yoghurt

① Mix all the dry ingredients together and add the oil. Warm the milk and yoghurt in a saucepan until hand-hot (it will curdle, but don't worry). Pour this into the dry ingredients and mix to form a soft, slightly sticky dough.

② Turn out on to a floured surface and knead for 5 minutes. Alternatively, put everything in a food processor and run the machine for 1 minute.

③ Put the dough in an oiled polythene bag and leave in a warm place for 1 hour to rise.

④ Knock back (punch down) the dough. Cut into six pieces and roll each into a ball, then roll out to a teardrop shape, about 12.5 cm/5 in long.

⑤ Place each one on a square of oiled foil, large enough to wrap it loosely. Draw the foil up over the dough and seal the edges, forming loose purses with room for the dough to rise.Transfer to a steamer in two tiers, cover with a lid and steam for 15 minutes.

⑥ Cook under a hot grill (broiler) for about 1 minute on each side until lightly browned in places. Serve warm.

PREPARATION AND COOKING TIME: ABOUT 30 MINUTES PLUS RISING

Steamed fruit cake
SERVES 8

For added texture, replace 50 g/2 oz/⅓ cup of the mixed dried fruit (fruit cake mix) with chopped mixed nuts.

100 g/4 oz/½ cup soft tub margarine
100 g/4 oz/½ cup soft light brown sugar
2 eggs
30 ml/2 tbsp milk
2.5 ml/½ tsp gravy browning (optional)
275 g/10 oz/2½ cups plain (all-purpose) flour
10 ml/2 tsp baking powder
5 ml/1 tsp mixed (apple-pie) spice
5 ml/1 tsp ground cinnamon
350 g/12 oz/2 cups mixed dried fruit (fruit cake mix)
15 g/½ oz/1 tbsp demerara sugar, to decorate

① Put all the ingredients in a large bowl and beat with a wooden spoon or an electric beater for about 3 minutes until smooth and well blended.

② Grease an 18 cm/7 in deep, round cake tin (pan) or soufflé dish and line the base with greased greaseproof (waxed) paper. Spoon in the mixture and level the surface. Cover with greased foil with a large pleat in the middle to allow for expansion. Twist and fold round the edges to secure or tie with string.

③ Transfer to a steamer, cover with a lid and steam for 2 hours. Remove from the steamer and sprinkle with the demerara sugar. Leave to cool for 15 minutes.

④ Loosen the edge, remove from the tin or dish, discard the cooking paper and leave to cool completely on a wire rack.

PREPARATION AND COOKING TIME: 2 HOURS 20 MINUTES

Spiced carrot and walnut cake

SERVES 8

---

175 g/6 oz/³/₄ cup butter or margarine, softened
100 g/4 oz/¹/₂ cup soft light brown sugar
60 ml/4 tbsp golden (light corn) syrup
175 g/6 oz/1¹/₂ cups self-raising (self-rising) flour
5 ml/1 tsp ground mixed (apple-pie) spice
2.5 ml/¹/₂ tsp bicarbonate of soda (baking soda)
2 large carrots, finely grated
1 egg, beaten
100 g/4 oz/1 cup chopped walnuts, plus a few for decoration
5 ml/1 tsp vanilla essence (extract)
150 g/5 oz/scant 1 cup icing (confectioners') sugar
Finely grated rind and juice of 1 small lemon or orange

---

① Put 100 g/4 oz/¹/₂ cup of the butter or margarine in a large bowl with all the ingredients except the icing sugar and lemon. Beat thoroughly with a wooden spoon until well blended.

② Grease a 18 cm/7 in cake tin (pan) or soufflé dish and line the base with a circle of greased greaseproof (waxed) paper. Turn the mixture into the tin or dish. Cover with greased foil with a pleat in the centre to allow for rising. Twist and fold round the edges to secure or tie with string.

③ Transfer to a steamer, cover with a lid and steam for 2 hours or until the centre springs back when pressed.

④ Leave to cool in the tin or dish for 30 minutes, then loosen the edge, turn out on to a wire rack, remove the paper and leave to cool completely.

⑤ Beat the remaining butter or margarine with the icing sugar, citrus rind and juice until smooth. Spread over the top of the cake. Sprinkle with a few chopped walnuts to decorate.

PREPARATION AND COOKING TIME: 2 HOURS 20 MINUTES

Cherry mallow cookie bars
MAKES 10

You can save time and effort by buying baby cooking marshmallows which don't need cutting up.

75 g/3 oz/⅓ cup butter or margarine, plus extra for greasing
1 egg
75 g/3 oz/⅓ cup caster (superfine) sugar
2.5 ml/½ tsp vanilla essence (extract)
175 g/6 oz/1 small packet of biscuits (cookies), such as Rich Tea
100 g/4 oz marshmallows
50 g/2 oz/½ cup glacé (candied) cherries, quartered

① Grease an 18 cm/7 in square shallow baking tin (pan) and line the base with greased greaseproof (waxed) paper.

② Put the butter or margarine in a bowl over a pan of gently simmering water or in the rice bowl of an electric steamer. Stir until melted.

③ Whisk in the egg, sugar and vanilla essence until thoroughly blended, then continue to steam, whisking occasionally for about 10 minutes or until slightly thickened.

④ Meanwhile, crush the biscuits in a bag with a rolling pin. Using wet scissors, snip the marshmallows into small pieces.

⑤ Remove the thickened mixture from the heat. Stir in the crushed biscuits, the marshmallows and the cherries. The marshmallows will partially melt.

⑥ Press the mixture into the prepared tin. Leave to cool, then chill.

⑦ Cut into bars before serving.

PREPARATION AND COOKING TIME: 20 MINUTES PLUS CHILLING

Chocolate-smothered mocha ring
SERVES 6–8

This moist cake has a truffle-like quality, making it rich and totally irresistible. It also makes a delicious dessert – simply fill the centre with whipped cream.

175 g/6 oz/1½ cups plain (semi-sweet) chocolate
50 g/2 oz/¼ cup butter or margarine, plus extra for greasing
50 g/2 oz/¼ cup caster (superfine) sugar
1 large egg, separated
6.5 ml/1¼ tsp instant coffee granules
10 ml/2 tsp hot water
75 g/3 oz/1½ cups fresh white breadcrumbs
50 g/2 oz/½ cup self-raising (self-rising) flour
90 ml/6 tbsp milk
25 g/1 oz/3 tbsp icing (confectioners') sugar

① Grease a 1 litre/1¾ pt/4¼ cup fluted ring mould and line the base with a ring of greased greaseproof (waxed) paper.

② Break up 50 g/2 oz/½ cup of the chocolate and melt in a bowl over a pan of gently simmering water.

③ Beat the butter or margarine and sugar together until light and fluffy. Beat in the melted chocolate and egg yolk. Dissolve 5 ml/1 tsp of the coffee in 5 ml/1 tsp of the water and stir in.

④ Add half the breadcrumbs, half the flour and half the milk. Fold in with a metal spoon. Add the remainder and fold in again.

⑤ Whisk the egg white until stiff and fold in with a metal spoon.

⑥ Turn into the prepared mould and level the surface. Cover with foil. Twist and fold all round to secure or tie with string.

⑦ Transfer to a steamer, cover with a lid and steam for 45–50 minutes or until firm to the touch.

⑧ Leave the cake to cool slightly, then turn out on to a wire rack and leave to cool completely.

⑨ Melt the remaining chocolate as before and spoon all over the top. Quickly spread it down the sides. Blend the remaining coffee with the remaining water and stir in the icing sugar. Using a teaspoon, trickle the icing over the cake in a haphazard pattern, to decorate. Leave to set.

PREPARATION AND COOKING TIME: ABOUT 1 HOUR

Chocolate rum truffles
MAKES ABOUT 24

I like to use bitter, very dark chocolate for this recipe. You can make white chocolate truffles in the same way.

150 g/5 oz/1¼ cups plain (semi-sweet) chocolate
1 egg yolk
15 g/½ oz/1 tbsp butter or margarine, softened
30 ml/2 tbsp double (heavy) cream
15 ml/1 tbsp rum
225 g/8 oz/1⅓ cups icing (confectioners') sugar, sifted
About 25 g/1 oz/¼ cup cocoa (unsweetened chocolate) powder

① Break up the chocolate and place it in a double saucepan, or in a bowl over a pan of gently simmering water, or in the rice bowl of an electric steamer. Stir occasionally until melted. Beat in the egg yolk.

② Remove the bowl from the heat and beat in the butter, cream and rum until smooth.

③ Gradually work in the icing sugar until the mixture forms a paste. Cover and chill for 2 hours.

④ Roll the mixture into 24 small balls. Roll each one in cocoa powder, then place in petit fours cases and chill until ready to serve.

PREPARATION AND COOKING TIME: 15 MINUTES PLUS CHILLING

Golden almond squares

MAKES UP TO 15

You can also steam these in a bain marie (see page 7)

A little oil, for greasing
100 g/4 oz/1 cup self-raising (self-rising) flour
5 ml/1 tsp baking powder
50 g/2 oz/1 cup fresh white breadcrumbs
65 g/1½ oz/scant ⅓ cup demerara sugar
50 g/2 oz/½ cup ground almonds
1 egg, separated
2.5 ml/½ tsp almond essence (extract)
150 ml/¼ pt/⅔ cup milk
15 g/½ oz/2 tbsp toasted flaked (slivered) almonds

① Grease a 900 g/2 lb loaf tin (pan) that will fit in the steamer. Cut a strip of greaseproof (waxed) paper the width of the tin and long enough to come up the short sides (this will aid with lifting the finished cake out). Grease the paper and place in the tin.

② Mix the flour and baking powder in a bowl. Stir in the breadcrumbs, 50 g/2 oz/¼ cup of the sugar and the ground almonds.

③ Add the egg yolk, almond essence and milk and beat until smooth.

④ Whisk the egg white until stiff and fold in with a metal spoon.

⑤ Turn into the prepared tin and cover the tin with foil, twisting and folding under the rim to secure.

⑥ Transfer to a steamer, cover with a lid and steam for 30 minutes. Quickly sprinkle the top with the remaining sugar and almonds, then re-cover and steam for a further 30 minutes.

⑦ Remove the foil and leave in the tin for 15 minutes. Lift out on to a wire rack and leave to cool. Cut into squares and store in an airtight container.

PREPARATION AND COOKING TIME: 1 HOUR 10 MINUTES

Chocolate raisin morning coffee bars

MAKES 12

A little oil, for greasing
175 g/6 oz plain biscuits (cookies), such as Morning
  Coffee
75 g/3 oz/⅓ cup butter or margarine, cut into pieces
25 g/1 oz/2 tbsp soft light brown sugar
45 ml/3 tbsp golden (light corn) syrup
40 g/1½ oz/⅓ cup cocoa (unsweetened chocolate) powder
50 g/2 oz/⅓ cup raisins
175 g/6 oz/1 cup icing (confectioners') sugar
40 ml/2½ tbsp water

① Oil an 18 x 28 cm/7 x 11 in shallow baking tin (pan).

② Put the biscuits in a bag and crush with a rolling pin (not too finely).

③ Put the butter or margarine in a large bowl over a pan of simmering water or in the rice bowl of an electric steamer. Add the sugar and syrup and 25 g/1 oz/¼ cup of the cocoa powder. Stir until melted.

④ Remove from the heat and stir in the biscuits and raisins.

⑤ Press into the prepared tin, leave to cool, then chill until firm.

⑥ Sift the remaining cocoa with the icing sugar into a bowl. Stir in the water to form a smooth icing (frosting). Spread over the top of the biscuit mixture. Decorate with the prongs of a fork, then leave to set. Cut into fingers and store in an airtight container.

PREPARATION AND COOKING TIME: 15 MINUTES PLUS CHILLING

Sauces and Sundries

Steaming is the perfect way to make sauces. If you try making Hollandaise sauce, for instance, in a saucepan, you have to work very hard and very quickly to make sure it doesn't curdle and it's also quite difficult to keep it warm once cooked. That's why it's far better being made in a double saucepan or a bowl over a pan of simmering water, or in the rice bowl of an electric steamer. You can take as much time as you like to make it to perfection.

This chapter also contains recipes for steaming other treats, such as clotted cream and lemon curd, that simply can't be made properly any other way!

Keeping sauces warm

It's not always convenient to make sauces at the minute you want to use them. Your steamer provides an ideal way to keep them warm and in perfect condition until you want to use them. To keep non-egg-based sauces warm, leave the container over the steam, turn down the heat as low as possible (making sure there is plenty of water in the base). Cover the sauce with a lid. Leave until ready to serve, stirring occasionally.

Egg-based sauces, such as Hollandaise, are best left covered, away from the heat. Then, about five minutes before serving, put the container of sauce back over the steam and heat, stirring all the time. Take care not to overheat or the sauce will curdle.

Note: Mousseline sauces are not suitable for reheating. They are best served as soon as they are made or they lose their foamy quality.

Cooked mayonnaise

MAKES ABOUT 450 ML/¾ PT/2 CUPS

This recipe avoids the use of raw eggs, which should not be given to young children or the elderly. For a less strong flavour, substitute sunflower for half the olive oil, if you prefer.

5 ml/1 tsp cornflour (cornstarch)
5 ml/1 tsp water
2.5 ml/½ tsp salt
2.5 ml/½ tsp caster (superfine) sugar
2.5 ml/½ tsp made English or Dijon mustard
2 eggs
300 ml/½ pt/1¼ cups olive oil
20 ml/1½ tbsp lemon juice
Salt and white pepper

① Blend the cornflour with the water, salt, sugar and mustard in a bowl over a pan of simmering water or in the rice bowl of an electric steamer.

② Whisk in the eggs.

③ Gradually trickle the oil into the bowl, whisking all the time until very thick and pale.

④ Remove the bowl from the steamer and whisk in the lemon juice. Immediately stand the bowl in cold water to cool it quickly.

⑤ Pour the mayonnaise into a clean screw-topped jar and store in the fridge. Use within 1 month.

PREPARATION AND COOKING TIME: 10 MINUTES

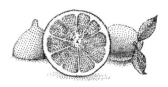

Hollandaise sauce

SERVES 4

Hollandaise has reputation for being tricky, but this method is the easiest I know.

2 eggs
A good pinch of cayenne
Salt and freshly ground black pepper
100 g/4 oz/¹/₂ cup butter, cut into small pieces
30 ml/2 tbsp lemon juice

① Using a balloon whisk or an electric beater, whisk the eggs with the cayenne and a pinch of salt and pepper in a bowl over a pan of simmering water or in the rice bowl of an electric steamer.

② Add the butter a piece or two at a time, whisking well after each addition until the mixture is thick and creamy. Add the lemon juice to taste and re-season, if necessary.

③ Keep warm until ready to serve.

PREPARATION AND COOKING TIME: 10–15 MINUTES

Béarnaise sauce

SERVES 4

If you can't get chervil, just use tarragon and parsley.

2 shallots or 1 small onion, finely chopped
45 ml/3 tbsp white wine vinegar
8 black peppercorns, coarsely crushed
2 egg yolks
100 g/4 oz/¹/₂ cup butter
5 ml/1 tsp each of chopped fresh tarragon, chervil and
    parsley

① Put the shallots or onion, vinegar and peppercorns in a small saucepan and boil for about 2 minutes, until the vinegar has reduced by half. Strain.

② Put the egg yolks in a bowl over a pan of simmering water or in the rice bowl of an electric steamer. Whisk in the strained vinegar and whisk for 1 minute.

③ Melt the butter and gradually add to the mixture, a little at a time, whisking well after each addition until thick and creamy. Stir in the herbs. Use as required.

PREPARATION AND COOKING TIME: 10–15 MINUTES

Savoury mousseline sauce
SERVES 4

This is lighter and fluffier than Hollandaise and is good with steamed vegetables, salmon and trout, in particular.

1 large egg
75 g/3 oz/⅓ cup unsalted (sweet) butter, cut into small pieces
15 ml/1 tbsp lemon or lime juice
Salt and freshly ground black pepper
60 ml/4 tbsp double (heavy) or whipping cream

① Put the egg in a bowl over a pan of simmering water or in the rice bowl of an electric steamer. Add two small pieces of the butter and whisk with a balloon whisk or electric beater until thick.

② Add the lemon juice and a little salt and pepper. Continue whisking, adding a knob of butter at a time until thick and creamy. Remove from the heat and whisk for a further minute.

③ Lightly whip the cream until softly peaking. Fold into the sauce, taste and re-season, if necessary.

PREPARATION AND COOKING TIME: 10–15 MINUTES

Custard

SERVES 4

2 eggs
15 ml/1 tbsp caster (superfine) sugar
300 ml/¹/₂ pt/1 ¹/₄ cups milk
A few drops of vanilla essence (extract)

① Whisk the eggs with the sugar and 45 ml/3 tbsp of the milk in a bowl that over a pan of simmering water, or in a double saucepan or the rice bowl of an electric steamer.

② Warm the remaining milk in a saucepan. Do not boil. Whisk into the egg mixture. Place over the simmering water and steam, whisking all the time until thick enough to coat the back of a spoon. Flavour to taste with vanilla essence.

③ Serve hot or cold.

PREPARATION AND COOKING TIME: 20 MINUTES

Rum custard sauce

SERVES 4

2 eggs
15 ml/1 tbsp caster (superfine) sugar
200 ml/7 fl oz/scant 1 cup milk
60 ml/4 tbsp single (light) cream
30 ml/2 tbsp rum

① Whisk the eggs with the sugar and 45 ml/3 tbsp of the milk in a bowl over a pan of simmering water, or in a double saucepan or the rice bowl of an electric steamer.

② Warm the remaining milk and cream in a saucepan. Do not boil. Whisk into the egg mixture with the rum. Place over the simmering water and steam, whisking all the time until thick enough to coat the back of a spoon.

④ Serve warm.

PREPARATION AND COOKING TIME: 20 MINUTES

Brandy sabayon
SERVES 4–6

3 egg yolks
30 ml/2 tbsp caster (superfine) sugar
150 ml/¼ pt/⅔ cup brandy

① Put all the ingredients in a bowl over a pan of simmering water, or in a double saucepan or the rice bowl of an electric steamer.

② Whisk with an electric beater or balloon whisk until thick and foamy. Use as soon as possible.

PREPARATION AND COOKING TIME: 5–10 MINUTES

Orange mousseline sauce
SERVES 4

You can make Lemon Mousseline Sauce, by substituting a lemon for the orange. For a special treat, make an alcoholic version, using 30 ml/2 tbsp orange, peach or coffee liqueur instead of the orange rind and juice.

2 small eggs
40 g/1½ oz/3 tbsp caster (superfine) sugar
Finely grated rind and juice of 1 orange

① Put all the ingredients in a bowl over a pan of simmering water or in a double saucepan or the rice bowl of an electric steamer.

② Whisk with an electric beater or hand whisk until thick and frothy.

③ Use immediately. It is delicious with steamed puddings or spooned over fresh soft fruits.

PREPARATION AND COOKING TIME: 5–10 MINUTES

Lemon curd
MAKES ABOUT 450 G/1 LB

For Orange Curd, use 2 oranges and 1 lemon instead of 3 lemons.

100 g/4 oz/¹/₂ cup unsalted (sweet) butter, cut into pieces
225 g/8 oz/1 cup granulated sugar
3 large eggs, beaten
Finely grated rind and juice of 3 large lemons

① Put all the ingredients in a bowl over a pan of simmering water, or in a double saucepan or the rice bowl of an electric steamer.

② Cook, stirring frequently, until the sugar melts and the curd thickens and will coat the back of the spoon – this should take about 30 minutes.

③ Pot, cover, cool and store. It will keep for up to 2 weeks in a cool, dry cupboard, and 1 month in the fridge.

PREPARATION AND COOKING TIME: 35 MINUTES

Hot chocolate sauce
SERVES 4

100 g/4 oz/1 cup plain (semi-sweet) chocolate
15 g/¹/₂ oz/1 tbsp butter or margarine
30 ml/2 tbsp icing (confectioners') sugar
45–60 ml/3–4 tbsp hot water

① Break up the chocolate and put in a bowl over a pan of simmering water or in a double saucepan or the rice bowl of an electric steamer. Steam until melted, stirring occasionally.

② Add the butter or margarine and icing sugar and stir all the time until smooth and well blended. Thin with hot water to the consistency you like. Serve hot.

PREPARATION AND COOKING TIME: 5–10 MINUTES

Pear, apple and cinnamon spread
MAKES ABOUT 450 G/1 LB

This can be made at the same time when you are steaming a pudding or something that takes a while. It's delicious on bread or toast and fabulous as a filling for sponge cakes.

3 eating (dessert) apples, peeled
3 ripe pears, peeled
15 ml/1 tbsp soft dark brown sugar
2.5 ml/½ tsp ground cinnamon
5 ml/1 tsp lemon juice
Clear honey, to taste
7.5 ml/1½ tsp powdered gelatine

① Thinly slice the apples and pears. Mix with the sugar, cinnamon and lemon juice in a bowl that will fit in a steamer.

② Transfer to the steamer, cover and steam for 1½ hours or until really pulpy, stirring once or twice.

③ Whisk in the gelatine until dissolved. Turn the mixture into a clean jar or container with a sealable lid. Cover, cool, then chill until set. It will keep in the fridge for up to 1 month.

PREPARATION AND COOKING TIME: 1 HOUR 40 MINUTES PLUS CHILLING

Golden brandy sauce
SERVES 4

Serve this sauce over ice cream or with steamed puddings.

90 ml/6 tbsp clear honey
45 ml/3 tbsp brandy
25 g/1 oz/2 tbsp unsalted (sweet) butter

① Put the honey and brandy in a bowl over a pan of simmering water, or in a double saucepan or the rice bowl of an electric steamer. Heat, stirring, until very hot.

② Whisk in the butter a small piece at a time until shiny and well blended. Serve hot.

PREPARATION AND COOKING TIME: 5–10 MINUTES

Clotted cream

MAKES ABOUT 225 G/8 OZ/1 CUP

Don't waste the leftover skimmed milk – you can use it in recipes for sauces or scones.

300 ml/¹/₂ pt/1 ¹/₄ cups milk
300 ml/¹/₂ pt/1 ¹/₄ cups single, whipping or double (heavy) cream

① Put the milk and cream in a wide, shallow, heatproof bowl that will fit in or over a steamer, or the rice bowl of an electric steamer. Leave in the fridge for at least 12 hours to allow the cream to rise to the surface.

② Transfer to a steamer and steam, uncovered, for 2 hours until a thick, golden crust forms on top.

③ Carefully remove the bowl from the steamer, leave to cool, then chill. Skim off the clotted cream using a draining spoon and store in a clean covered pot in the fridge.

PREPARATION AND COOKING TIME: 2 HOURS
PLUS STANDING AND CHILLING

Low-fat thick clotted cream

MAKES ABOUT 200 G/7 OZ/SCANT 1 CUP

I discovered this by mistake one day when I was trying to make a low-fat version using cream substitute, but forgot to add any milk. The result was fantastic!

250 ml/8 fl oz/1 cup low-fat double (heavy) cream

① Pour the low-fat cream into a wide, shallow heatproof bowl that will fit in or over a steamer or in the rice bowl of an electric steamer. Steam for 2–3 hours.

③ Remove the bowl from the heat and leave to cool, then chill. Gently break up the crust and fold it into the thick cream below. Store in a clean covered pot in the fridge.

PREPARATION AND COOKING TIME: 2–3 HOURS PLUS CHILLING

Index